# USING FASTBACK® PLUS

# USING FASTBACK® PLUS

## Kate Lee Johnson

**Addison-Wesley Publishing Company, Inc.**
Reading, Massachusetts  Menlo Park, California  New York
Don Mills, Ontario  Wokingham, England  Amsterdam  Bonn  Sydney
Singapore  Tokyo  Madrid  San Juan

Copyright © 1990 Benchmark Productions
ISBN: 0-201-57045-9

Production Editor: Amorette Pedersen
Cover Design by Mike Fender
Set in 11-point Palatino by Benchmark Productions

ABCDEFGHIJ-MW-943210
First Printing, June 1990

This book is lovingly dedicated to Eliza, whose stoic willingness to fill in for me as "the Mommy" made it possible.

# Table of Contents

# About This Book

Using FASTBACK PLUS is designed to help both beginning and experienced computer users get the most out of FASTBACK PLUS. It is organized in a straightforward manner:

Part I contains conceptual background material to help you understand the whys and wherefores of using FASTBACK PLUS to protect your valuable computer files.

Part II provides reference information to help you learn to navigate and use the FASTBACK PLUS menu system.

Part III contains step-by-step tutorials on executing the following common FASTBACK PLUS procedures:

- Backing up your hard disk files.
- Restoring backup files to the hard disk.
- Backing up only recently changed files.
- Hand-selecting the files you want to backup or restore.
- Saving and replaying frequently-used keystroke sequences and menu settings.

Part IV offers more information on automating your backup routines and using some of FASTBACK PLUS's advanced features.

At the end of the book, you will find a set of appendices with information on:

- Installing FASTBACK PLUS
- FASTBACK PLUS Error Messages
- A Glossary of Terms
- Tips for Users of Original FASTBACK and FASTBACK II

Use this book in good health, and may you never have to do an emergency restore!

*PART I*

# Introduction to FASTBACK PLUS

Since its introduction in 1984, FASTBACK is a name that has deservedly become equated with the rapid and reliable backup of valuable information stored on personal computer hard disks.

FASTBACK PLUS is the newest version (2.01) of this well-known software package from Fifth Generation Systems. It offers an impressive array of features that not only make backing up your hard disk fast, simple, and efficient, but also allow you to customize a convenient backup routine that fits neatly into your regular work habits, rather than forcing you to adopt a rigid backup strategy.

What sets FASTBACK PLUS apart from other, run-of-the-mill programs? To answer that question, we should examine some of the concepts and issues involved in disk backup.

# CHAPTER 1

# *Why Make Backups?*

A look at the nature of personal computers and computerized recordkeeping reveals several important reasons for backing up your hard disk.

## The Risk of Data Loss

The most obvious reason for making backups of your hard disk is *security*. It's a dangerous world for hard disks—many possibilities for losing your valuable data lurk around every corner, any one of which can literally wipe out weeks, months, or even years of work and leave you high and dry with your customers, vendors, or just personal recordkeeping. Here is the "most wanted" list of threats to your hard disk:

### Head Crash

A simple analogy for the way your hard disk can be damaged in a head crash is an old-fashioned record player. You put a record on the turntable, start it spinning, set the needle down on the surface of the record, and out comes sound. Everything is fine as long as the turntable doesn't get jostled or bumped—but as soon as that happens, the needle skids across the record, making a big scratch along the way and rendering the record unplayable.

Your hard disk operates in a similar, if not entirely comparable, manner. The surfaces of the disk are coated with a special magnetic recording material, which can be "read" and "written to" by magnetic *heads* floating only a few thousandths of an inch away from those surfaces. These delicately suspended heads move back and forth across the disk's surfaces, never actually touching the surfaces themselves, to read and write bits of data as you work on your computer.

Like the case of the turntable, as long as nothing happens to jar your computer or cause the hard disk to malfunction, your data is perfectly safe. However, if something goes wrong, as it easily can, the magnetic head can actually touch the magnetic surface of the disk, causing both damage to the disk and loss of your data. While the disk can probably be repaired, your data may not fare so well. Without current disk backups, your data—not only where the head actually crashed, but any interdependent data at other disk locations as well—will probably be lost forever.

### Power Failure

Probably the most common threat to data on your hard disk is an unexpected loss of power. An electrical storm comes up out of nowhere while you are deeply engrossed in work for an important client...a tree falls on the wires three blocks away and the whole neighborhood loses power while you are sweating out the year-end financials for your business...someone in your house decides to work on an electrical fixture and throws the circuit breaker without checking to see that you are in the middle of your monthly accounts...

It happens to everyone at one time or another. Be prepared. If you make regular backups of your hard disk at frequent intervals, a power failure does not have to mean significant data loss.

### Accidental Erasure

"How could I be so stupid?" you wail, as you realize that you just erased the first six chapters of your novel.

Accidental erasure of data from a hard disk has no respect for computer expertise. It can happen to anyone, novice or pro. After all, everyone's mind is on something else at some time, and even experts occasionally run into unfamiliar terrain where accidents are more likely to happen.

And for each person who shares your computer environment, the odds are that much higher that eventually, an accident will take out some of your data.

### Theft or Damage

Personal computers are fairly popular burglary items. And while thieves are unlikely to be interested in your set of backup floppies, the data on your hard disk will go out the window with the computer—and no amount of insurance coverage can recover lost data.

Another possibility that most people don't even consider until the situation arises, is computer breakdown or damage of some kind that doesn't even affect your hard disk, but does cause your computer to end up "in the shop" at a time that happens to be critical to the work you are doing. You can borrow or rent another computer, but not a duplicate of your hard disk. With current backups, however, you just load the latest copy of your data into the temporary computer and go back to work.

## Strategic Considerations

The threat of data loss is a compelling argument all by itself for religiously keeping backups of your hard disk. But you don't necessarily need special software just to make backup disks. The decision to use backup software rather than relying on your operating system's copy commands, and the further decision of *which* backup software to use, hinge on other factors.

## Speed

Operating system utilities such as copying commands are designed to serve broad, generic purposes. Therefore, they don't necessarily provide the quickest or most efficient methods for accomplishing potentially time-consuming, specialized tasks like backing up an entire hard disk.

FASTBACK PLUS is highly optimized for speed. By making full use of Direct Memory Access—a technique for directly transferring data to and from disks under the control of a separate chip called the DMA chip— FASTBACK PLUS is able to read from one disk while simultaneously writing to another. This accounts for Fifth Generation Systems' confidence in the claim that FASTBACK PLUS is the "world's fastest" backup software. (Note: If you have not already installed FASTBACK PLUS on your computer, you will learn more about the DMA chip when you go through the installation process, which is described in Appendix A.)

## Disk Performance

The constant creation of new files and deletion of old files on your hard disk eventually results in a phenomenon called *disk fragmentation*. As you erase files, empty spaces are created on the disk, which then get filled up with pieces of other files as you modify or create them. Thus, before long, with files being saved in scattered bits and pieces all over the disk, your disk's performance can slow down considerably.

To restore your hard disk to an unfragmented state, you can periodically use FASTBACK PLUS to make an *extra* backup of all your files, then immediately reformat the disk and restore the files from the backups while they are still fresh. The restored files will be written onto the hard disk contiguously, thus eliminating disk fragmentation.

### File Archiving

Your files probably contain important records—home or business finances, client projects, works-in-progress. You may have neither the space on your hard disk nor the need to keep a lot old files current, but chances are you don't want to just get rid of them either.

FASTBACK PLUS is a great archiving tool. Because you have complete control over the selection of files to back up, you can use FASTBACK PLUS to make tailored backups of selected sets of old files. The files no longer take up precious space on your hard disk. But they will always be available should you need them.

And FASTBACK PLUS provides another valuable archiving service. For certain kinds of work, it can be very useful to have access to older versions of your files. For example, a writer might want to go back to an earlier version of a chapter if the current rewrite isn't turning out as planned. FASTBACK PLUS's *incremental backup* type can provide those needed older versions. We'll take a closer look at incremental backups and how they differ from both *full* and *differential* backups in Chapter 2.

### Rapid Data Duplication

Finally, your FASTBACK PLUS backup procedure can double as a rapid data duplication service when you need to distribute copies of new in-house programs or data sets to others in your office or group. Because backing up files with FASTBACK PLUS is so much faster than using the operating system's copying facilities, it makes sense to use FASTBACK PLUS when you need to distribute copied files quickly. Just make sure that everyone who receives your copied files also has a copy of FAST-BACK PLUS to restore them.

# CHAPTER 2

# *How FASTBACK PLUS Works*

FASTBACK PLUS is a straightforward, menu-based program. The Main menu contains three submenus:

- **Backup** The backup menu offers selections for specifying source (hard disk) and destination drives, selecting files to back up, and checking the set of files you have chosen before you start your backup.

- **Restore** The restore menu offers many of the same activities as the backup menu. The main difference is that the Restore procedure operates in the reverse direction; thus, the hard disk you specify will be the *destination*, and the floppy drive the *source*. A few additional selections are pertinent only when you are restoring files to disk, such as choosing history files and whether to allow files on the disk to be overwritten by restored files of the same name.

- **Options** The Options menu is where FASTBACK PLUS provides the bulk of its advanced features, including the abilities to change from Beginner level activities to more advanced, to save frequently used Backup and Restore routines in "setup files," and to automate your FASTBACK PLUS procedures by saving and re-playing keystroke macros, as well as quite a few others.

FASTBACK PLUS's menu structure is easy to navigate. In fact, most PC users will be able to use it right away to make full backups of their hard disks without learning a whole lot about the theory and practice of back-ups.

But if you want to take full advantage of FASTBACK PLUS's power and many features to fine-tune your backup strategy, it is worth spending a little time up front learning how FASTBACK PLUS does what it does, and how to get the most out of it.

This chapter gives you the conceptual background you need in order to understand exactly how FASTBACK PLUS works and why it works that way. This understanding will help you reap benefits you might not have imagined from using FASTBACK PLUS.

The following topics are covered:

- Backup methods
- Selecting a backup type
- Setting the user level
- Controlling file selection

Note: Part II of this book contains alphabetized summaries of FAST-BACK PLUS's menus, which describe and illustrate each menu selection in more detail.

## Backup Methods

FASTBACK PLUS derives its great flexibility from the fact that it uses the *file-oriented* backup method rather than the *disk image* method.

The disk image method takes a "snapshot" of your disk, so that when the files are restored, the disk returns to the exact condition it was in when the backup was made. Though the disk image is fast and clean, it does not allow you to do anything less than a full backup each time you use it. And watching the minutes tick by when you are late for an appointment, but don't want to leave important files unprotected, can be frustrating for any busy person.

Full backups are useful and necessary at certain intervals of course, but if you're backing up your hard disk every day that you use your computer—as you should!—you probably want to back up only those files that have changed since the last backup. This will save time (and also your work). With FASTBACK PLUS, you can be as selective as you need to be about which files you back up at any given time. So, as long as you are careful to schedule a full backup at appropriate intervals, your backup routine should remain convenient and manageable. (Chapter 3 offers some guidelines to help you establish the best backup routine for your situation.)

## Selecting a Backup Type

FASTBACK PLUS provides three main backup types. The first is a *full backup*. You should make a full backup periodically to ensure that you always have a complete and relatively current backup set.

The other two types, *differential* and *incremental*, are *partial* or *selected files* backups. You can use a partial backup to back up only those files you have edited or changed during your current session at the computer. An important distinction between the two partial backup types will become clear as you read about each in the sections that follow.

The availability of three different backup types in FASTBACK PLUS means you can mix and match to devise a backup strategy that is truly tailored to your needs.

### The Archive Flag

Before you can understand the differences among FASTBACK PLUS's three backup types, you need to understand how FASTBACK PLUS "keeps track" of which files have been backed up and what type of backup was used for each. It does this by means of the DOS *archive flag*.

The archive flag is a toggle setting associated with each file; it is initially set to 1. When DOS, or a backup utility such as FASTBACK PLUS, backs up a file, it normally sets the archive flag to 0, indicating that the file has been backed up. The next time you change the file, the flag is set back to 1.

FASTBACK PLUS exercises fine control over the use of the archive flag, as we shall see shortly, in order to provide the distinctions among its backup types.

### The History File

One further tool that FASTBACK PLUS uses is the *History File*. FAST-BACK PLUS records a complete catalog of all the files backed up in one backup set on your hard disk. The catalog includes information about each file, such as its name, size, date, and time it was last changed, volume and track numbers, and so on. The history file also includes identifying information assigned to the entire backup set by FASTBACK PLUS.

The FASTBACK PLUS Options menu allows you to view and to print history files, as well as get copies of history files from the floppy disk in case the files are damaged on the hard disk. History files are examined in more detail in Chapter 7.

### Full Backup

The full backup hardly needs explanation. FASTBACK PLUS simply makes a complete copy of the entire contents of your hard disk on as many floppy disks as are required to hold all the files. When the full backup is completed, you have a backup set from which you can restore all or part to your hard disk.

Note: as we mentioned earlier, restoring all of a full backup set—as long as it is *current*—will eliminate disk fragmentation and speed up your disk's performance.

Full backup is the FASTBACK PLUS default backup type. In the absence of other instructions, FASTBACK PLUS will assume you want a full backup.

### Partial Backups

Both the differential backup and the incremental backup are partial backups; that is, they back up only those files that have changed. The main difference between the two types is in the amount of elapsed time that each uses as the criterion for choosing the set of files it will back up.

**The Differential Backup**   This option selects all those files that have changed *since the last full backup*; regardless of whether individual files already have been backed up in an earlier differential backup. It does this because the differential backup does not reset the archive flag when it backs up a file. Therefore, each time you do a differential backup, FAST-BACK PLUS goes all the way back to the last full backup and makes a new backup copy of every file that has changed since.

Since all changed files back to the last full backup are copied anew each time, you can use the same disks over again each time you make a differential backup. This will save you some floppy disks. And although a differential backup may take a little longer overall, it does save FASTBACK PLUS having to format a new set of disks each time.

If you largely work on the same set of files every time you use your computer, you may prefer to use differential backups to supplement your full backups.

**The Incremental Backup**   This option selects only files that have changed *since the last incremental backup*. When you choose an incremental backup, FASTBACK PLUS literally backs up only those files whose archive flags have been *unset* by changes to the file. It then *sets* the archive flags of the files it has backed up so that the next time you do an incremental backup, those files won't be included unless they have been changed again in the meantime. Thus, each time you do an incremental backup, you are recording only those changes that have actually occurred on your hard disk since the last time you did an incremental backup. The rest don't get backed up again until you do an entirely new full backup.

When FASTBACK PLUS makes an incremental backup, it appends the backup's history file to the last full backup's history file. This gives you a continuing record of your backups between full backups. Also, if you choose to restore from your collected backups—both full and incremental—FASTBACK PLUS uses the combined history file to increase the efficiency of the restoration by automatically selecting only the most recent files. This is called a "smart" restore.

The incremental backup is a good partial backup type to use if you tend to work on different files each time you use your computer. It is also ideal for people who like to have access to earlier versions of their files, since each incremental backup set represents a different, later selection of files.

Normally, the incremental backup is faster than the differential simply because it backs up fewer files each time. Of course, using incremental backups means you have to use a new set of floppy disks for each one— at least until you do your next full backup. But it can be worth it to have the kind of version control that incremental backups provide. Figure 2-1 shows the differences between differential and incremental backups.

*Figure 2-1: Incremental versus Differential Backups*

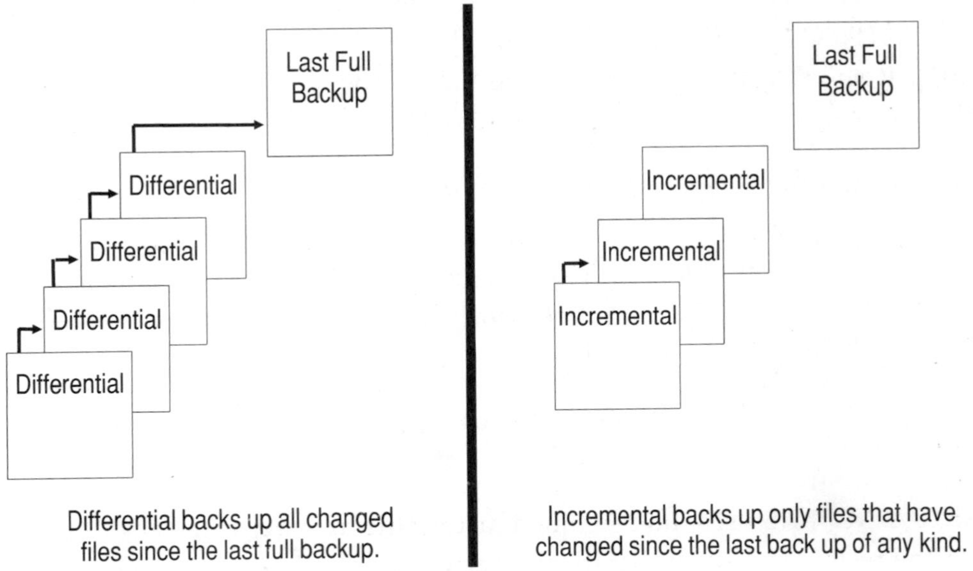

Differential backs up all changed files since the last full backup.

Incremental backs up only files that have changed since the last back up of any kind.

## Special Backup Types

In addition to the three main backup types described above, FASTBACK PLUS offers two special types of backup: the *Full Copy* and the *Separate Incremental*.

**The Full Copy**    The Full Copy backup operates exactly like the full backup except that it *does not set archive flags*. This makes it very useful for simply copying and distributing files without necessarily keeping a set of the disks as a backup.

**The Separate Incremental**    This type of backup is a true incremental backup except that its history file is not appended to the full backup. Thus, it can be restored separately from your full backup. This is useful if you want to restore interim versions of your files to your hard disk. An editor trying to maintain an edit trail of changes to files may find this option helpful.

## Advantages of Each Backup Type

Table 2-1 summarizes the main features, advantages, and disadvantages of each of FASTBACK PLUS's main backup types: Full, Differential, and Incremental. It should be helpful when the time comes to devise your own backup strategy a little later on (see Chapter 3).

*Table 2-1: FASTBACK PLUS Backup Types*

| Type | Features | Advantages | Disadvantages |
|---|---|---|---|
| Full | Automatically selects all files. FASTBACK PLUS default backup type. | Provides complete, current backup for restoration. Second full backup can be used to eliminate disk fragmentation. | Too time-consuming to do every day. Relying on full backup alone can cause confusion if you want to restore files to hard disk as each new full backup resets the archive flags, rendering previous full backups out of date. |
| Differential | Backs up all files that have changed since last full backup. Does not reset archive flags. | Can reuse same set of floppy disks each time. Good to use between full backups if you use same files each time you work. | Discards interim versions of your files unless you use a "rotation system" (see Chapter 3). Time-consuming unless you make frequent full backups. |

| Type | Features | Advantages | Disadvantages |
|------|----------|------------|---------------|
| Incremental | Backs up all files that have changed since last incremental backup. Resets archive flags of newly backed up files. | Good to use between full backups if you use different files each time you work. Preserves and allows you to restore all versions of files. Takes less time than differential backup, since it backs up fewer files each time. | Disk-consuming because you must use a new set of floppy disks for each new incremental backup. |

## Controlling the User Level

FASTBACK PLUS provides three user levels in its menu system: Beginner, Experienced, and Advanced. This allows each user to select the level appropriate to his or her own computer experience and knowledge of the operating system.

Selecting a user level automatically alters the menu choices available to you, depending on the level you choose. For example, at the Beginner level, only one method of file selection is available, to keep things simple. Experienced and Advanced users, on the other hand, can exercise quite a bit of control over how files are selected for backup.

Of course, you set the user level yourself, so you can set it at Advanced even if you are a novice computer user, or vice versa. But as a rule, it is best to stick to the simpler procedures provided at the Beginner level until you have gained the confidence that you need to really use the Experienced and Advanced features to your best advantage. You will certainly know when you have progressed beyond Beginner.

The default user level is Beginner. To change the user level to Experienced or Advanced, just select User Level from the Options menu and then select the level you want.

Table 2-2 summarizes the important differences among the three user levels. It shows all the activities available at the Beginner level. For the Experienced and Advanced levels, it shows only those activities that are *additional* features for that level.

*Table 2-2: User Levels and Features*

| User Level | Backup Menu | Restore Menu | Options |
|---|---|---|---|
| Beginner | Identify hard disk. | Identify target hard disk. | Set user level. |
| | Choose files to back up. | Choose files to restore. | Install FASTBACK PLUS. |
| | Specify destination drive. | Specify source drive. | View or print history reports. |
| | Select backup type. | Create directories on hard disk (if needed). | Save and load setup files. |
| | Preview file selection before backup. | | |
| | Start backup. | | |
| Experienced | Select files by marking for Include (same as Choose Files at Beginner level) or Exclude. | Control selection of history files. | Delete or Save old history reports. |
| | | Select files by Include or Exclude. | Control write verification. |
| | | Control whether FASTBACK PLUS overwrites existing files of same name when restoring files to hard disk. | Control overwrite warning for used disks. |
| | | | Control audible prompts. |

| User Level | Backup Menu | Restore Menu | Options |
|---|---|---|---|
| | | | Control screen colors. |
| | | | Pause to use MS-DOS command. |
| | | | Save and play back keystroke macros. |
| Advanced | Select files to back up by date. | Select files to restore by date. | Tell FASTBACK PLUS whether or not to format backup disks. |
| | | Control Archive Flag setting. | Control data compression. |
| | | Control individual file and directory selection. | Control error correction. |
| | | | Use Password protection. |

## Controlling File Selection

When you use one of FASTBACK PLUS's predetermined backup types—Full, Differential, or Incremental—you do not need to select files. FASTBACK PLUS automatically selects files to back up according to how the archive flag is set for each file. You simply select the backup type you want, and FASTBACK PLUS does all the file selection.

Under many circumstances however, you may want to tell FASTBACK PLUS exactly which files you want to include in a backup or restore procedure. Depending on the user level you choose, FASTBACK PLUS gives you a great deal of control and flexibility in identifying exactly the set of files you wish to include.

### File Selection Filters

FASTBACK PLUS provides three *filters* to help you define the set of files you want to back up or restore. They are available as menu selections on the Backup and Restore menus.

**Choose Files**   At the Beginner level, the Backup and Restore menus offer only one filter for selecting files: **Choose Files**. Choose Files allows you to actively identify each directory, partial directory, or individual file you want to include in the list of files you will back up or restore. Figure 2-2 shows the Choose Files filter on the Beginner menu.

**Include Files**   The Experienced and Advanced menus also offer the Choose Files filter, only under a different name: **Include Files**. Include Files works exactly the same way as Choose Files; there is no difference except in the name. Figure 2-3 shows the Include Files filter on the Experienced and Advanced menus.

**Exclude Files**   Both the Experienced and Advanced menus also offer another filter: **Exclude Files**. You use the same methods of file selection you use with Include Files. The difference is that Exclude Files creates a list of files to be *excluded* from your backup or restore procedure. Figure 2-4 shows the Exclude Files filter on Experienced and Advanced menus.

You typically use Exclude Files to modify selections you have made with Include Files by excluding individual files or subgroups from a larger group of files. For example, you might want to back up all of the files in one directory except for a certain group that you know you haven't changed. In this case, you might use Include Files to insert the full directory in the list with a wildcard file designation:

```
\WP\CORSPND\*.*
```

And then use Exclude Files to exclude only the memos in that directory, which have a filename extension of .MEM:

```
\WP\CORSPND\*.MEM
```

*Figure 2-2: Choosing Files on the Beginner Menu*

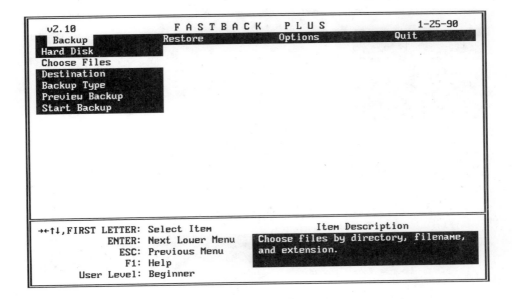

*Figure 2-3: Include Files on the Experience/Advanced Menus*

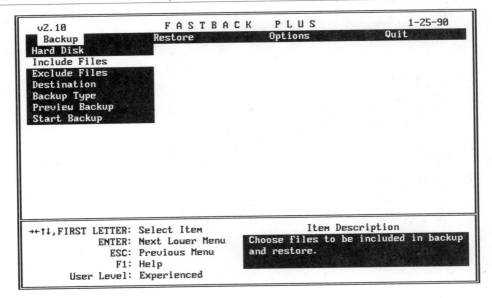

*Figure 2-4: Exclude Files on the Experienced/Advanced Menus*

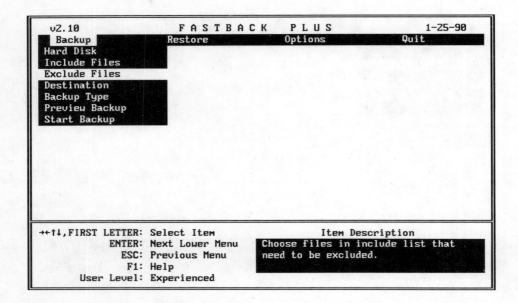

Note that you do not need to explicitly add files to your Exclude list that you have not included with Include Files; FASTBACK PLUS automatically excludes anything not explicitly included.

**Files by Date**   The Advanced menu offers one final file selection filter, which allows you to further narrow the set of files you want to back up or restore: **Files by Date**. Like Exclude Files, you use Files by Date after you have made your list of files to Include (and Exclude). Figure 2-5 shows the Files by Date filter on the Advanced menu.

A series of prompts guides you through the creation of a Date Gate. The Date Gate excludes files created before and after certain dates that FAST-BACK PLUS prompts you to specify. Thus, you can narrow down the files on your Include list to only those files that were created within the specified period, or "Date Gate." That gate is shown in Figure 2-6.

*Figure 2-5: Files by Date on the Advanced Menu*

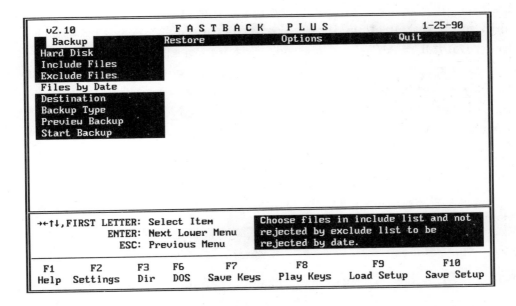

*Figure 2-6: Creation of a Date Gate*

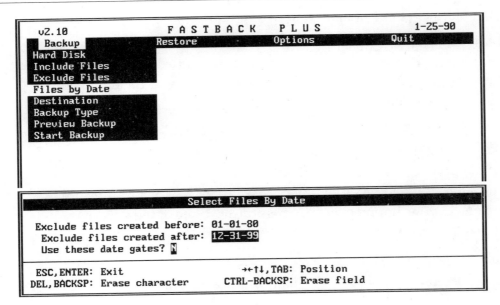

After prompting you to specify the before and after dates of the Date Gate, FASTBACK PLUS asks if you want to "Use these date gates?" At first glance, this may seem like a rhetorical question. After all, why would you go to the trouble of creating a Date Gate if you didn't intend to use it? But it turns out there is a good reason for asking this question: if some of your files have no creation date associated with them, perhaps because they were imported from another system, you can prevent them from slipping through the cracks by answering N for No to this prompt. If you want the dates to apply to *all* your files, answer Y for Yes and FASTBACK PLUS will ignore the files with no dates.

FASTBACK PLUS's combination of Include Files, Exclude Files, and Files by Date gives you a very fine degree of control over file selection for both backup and restore procedures.

### File Selection Methods

Files by Date is a special case of file selection, with its series of prompts. The other file selection filters described above offer two basic methods of choosing the files and directories you want to add to your list.

When you use the Choose Files selection from the Beginner level Backup or Restore menu, or the Include Files or Exclude Files selections from the Experienced and Advanced menus, a window entitled **Choose Files To Include** appears at the bottom of your screen, below the menu. Figure 2-7 shows this window.

This is where FASTBACK PLUS lists the files you select for your current backup or restore procedure. Notice that the source drive is identified in the top, left-hand corner of the window. In the case of a backup, this will be the letter designation of your hard disk; in the case of a restore, it will name one of your floppy drives. Across the next line of the window, you see the following columns:

- # The line number. The window has 20 lines.
- **Directories:** The directory name for the current line.

- **Files:** The name of a file or group of files (via wildcard designations).
- **Include Subdirs:** Whether to include all subdirectories of this directory. The default is Y (Yes). If you want to ignore subdirectories of a particular directory, change the Y to N.

*Figure 2-7: The Choose Files To Include Window*

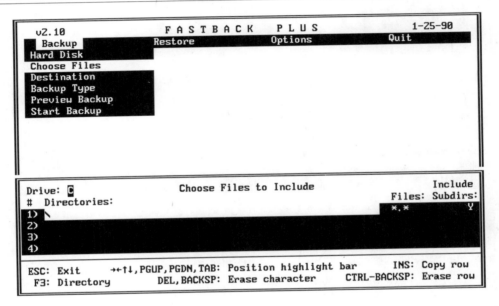

FASTBACK PLUS provides two methods of adding files to this list:

**Pathname**  You can type the full pathname of any file or group of files right into the list, using wildcards (*.*) to add whole directories or subgroups. Figure 2-8 shows a screen with a sample pathname.

The pathname consists of:

- The full directory name, including any subdirectories. For example, \BUSINESS\SPREADSHEETS\MONTHLY
- The filename or names. For example, MARCH.FIN for a single file, or *.FIN for all files in that directory with a file extension of

.FIN, or MARCH.* for all files containing information about the
month of March, but having different file extensions.

*Figure 2-8: A Pathname*

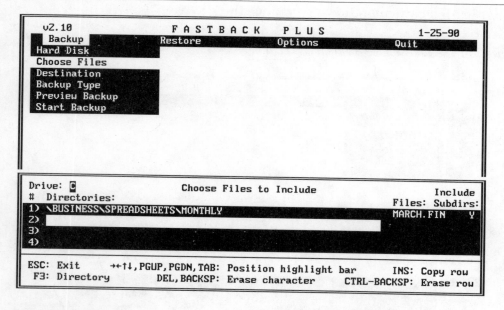

**A Note About DOS Pathnames**   DOS uses *pathnames* to specify the location of
a file on a disk. A pathname consists of:

- The single-letter drive designation followed by a colon (:)
- A backslash (\) character, which designates the *root* or top-level
  directory on your computer.
- A directory name followed by another backslash.
- Any subdirectory names (directories within directories) sepa-
  rated by more backslashes.
- A filename—usually up to eight letters and numbers, followed by
  a period (.), followed by a three-letter *extension*, which indicates
  what type of file it is.

Here is an example of a typical DOS hard disk pathname:

```
C:\BUSINESS\SPREADSHEETS\MONTHLY\MARCH.FIN
```

Asterisks (*), referred to as *wildcard characters*, can be used in place of the different filename components to indicate any characters that fit the rest of the filename description. For example, the following filename indicates all files with an extension of FIN:

```
*.FIN
```

The next example, on the other hand, indicates all files with the name "March", regardless of extension:

```
MARCH.*
```

A wildcard string, *.*, indicates "all files in the designated directory."

For more information on DOS pathnames and filenames, consult your DOS manual.

Notice that FASTBACK PLUS has automatically inserted a default pathname of \*.* with a Y under Include Subdirectories. The \ stands for your *root directory* (top-level directory that contains all other directories) and the *.* for all files in that directory. FASTBACK PLUS's default pathname specifies all files in your root directory, including all sub-directories of the root. Figure 2-9 shows the FASTBACK PLUS window with the default pathname. This is the specification for a full backup of your hard disk.

If you want to select files, you can start by editing this default pathname. A chart at the bottom of the Choose Files To Include window shows the keys you can use to move around and edit lines in the window. Note that the TAB key, not the ENTER key, moves you across the columns in this window.

*Figure 2-9: The FASTBACK PLUS Default Pathname*

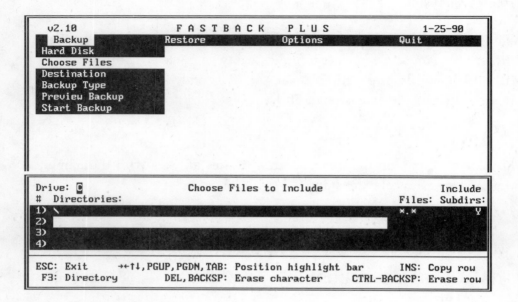

If you would rather not enter files by typing their pathnames, you can select files by a second method, called the *Directory Tree*, by pressing F3.

**Directory Tree**   A directory tree is a graphical display of a directory and its subdirectories. It appears at the top of your screen when you press F3, temporarily replacing the FASTBACK PLUS menu. Figure 2-10 shows a sample hard disk directory tree.

As the new key mapping at the bottom of your screen indicates (see Figure 2-10), you can use the arrow keys to scroll both vertically and horizontally through the directory tree.

To include a whole directory in your list of files, just highlight that directory and press INS. Figure 2-11 shows the directory tree with a highlighted directory. FASTBACK PLUS automatically copies the directory name with a wildcard file designation into the next available line of the Choose Files To Include window.

*Figure 2-10: A Hard Disk Directory Tree*

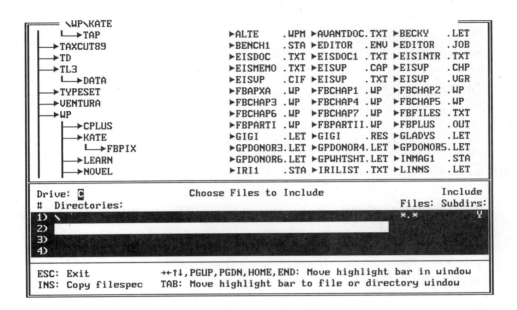

*Figure 2-11: Highlighted Directory Added to File List*

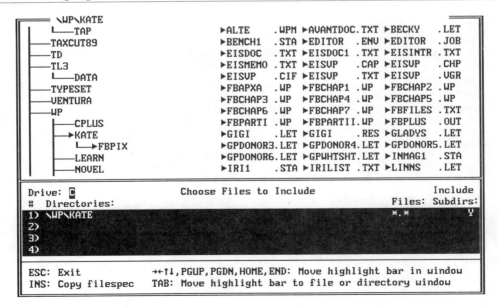

To insert only part of a directory into the Choose Files To Include window, you must use a combination of methods, following these steps:

- Step 1: Press F3 to get the directory tree.
- Step 2: Highlight the directory you want in the directory tree and press INS.
- Step 3: Press ESC to exit the directory tree and to activate the Choose Files To Include window.
- Step 4: Edit the wildcard file designation to include only the files you actually want to list from the named directory. A sample partial file designation is shown in Figure 2-12. (For example, if you give all your text files a file extension of .TXT, and you want only the text files from this directory, you would change the wildcard filename to read: *.TXT.)

Using the directory tree to insert individual files in the Choose Files To Include window is also easy.

*Figure 2-12: Including a Partial Directory*

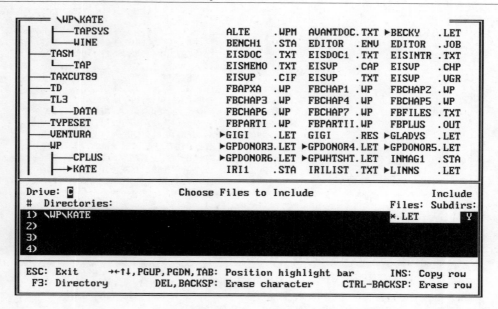

When a directory is highlighted, its files are listed to the right of the tree. To add individual files to your list, first press TAB to switch the highlight bar to the files list. Then you can scroll through the files list and select individual files by highlighting them and pressing INS. Figure 2-13 shows the selection of individual files. Again, FASTBACK PLUS copies the pathname of the file into the Choose Files To Include window. You can switch back to the directory tree anytime by pressing TAB again.

*Figure 2-13: Selecting Individual Files*

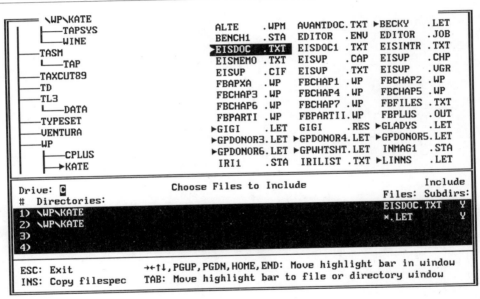

**Include Subdirectories**   The Include Subdirs: column in the Choose Files To Include window requires only a (Y) Yes or (N) No answer. The default is Y, which tells FASTBACK PLUS to include all subdirectories of the designated directory, using exactly the same file specification for each subdirectory.

For any line in which you put an N in the Include Subdirs: column, FASTBACK PLUS ignores subdirectories.

### Saving Your List of Files

To save your list of files and leave the Choose Files To Include window, press ESC. This takes you back to the FASTBACK PLUS menu, where you can proceed with your backup or restore procedure.

# CHAPTER 3

# *Establishing a Backup Strategy*

There is no question that regular backups of your hard disk can save you untold time, headaches, and very likely money, if anything should go wrong. The only real question is how you define "regular"—and that depends on how often you use your computer.

If you are a daily computer user, then you should be a daily backup maker. It's as simple as that.

To most people, taking the time to make daily backups of their hard disk sounds like a lot more trouble than it's worth. But consider these facts:

1. It is impossible to gauge how much a current backup is worth until disaster strikes.
2. You have already accepted the need to back up your hard disk at least once in a while, or you wouldn't be reading this book.
3. FASTBACK PLUS will probably surprise you very pleasantly with its potential for automated backup routines. Once you have mastered some of FASTBACK PLUS's advanced features, a daily backup routine will no longer seem like a chore you would just as soon skip.

Obviously, however, making a daily backup is not going to fit unobtrusively into your routine if you have to take the time to make a *full* backup each time. True, FASTBACK PLUS is very fast, but a full backup is still not something everyone longs to do daily.

That is where FASTBACK PLUS's partial backup types come in. You can start out with one full backup of your entire hard disk. Then make either differential or incremental daily backups until the next time you make a full backup.

Here are some questions to consider when you try to establish your backup strategy:

How often should I make a full backup?

Again, that is up to you and your routines, but once every week or two is probably best.

How do I choose between differential and incremental backup types for my daily backups?

Remember that Differential backups make new backups of every file that has changed *since the last full backup*, regardless of whether the file was backed up in yesterday's differential backup and hasn't changed since.

In contrast, Incremental backups make new backups of only those files that have changed *since the last incremental backup*. Thus, only the files you have actually changed *today* are backed up (assuming you did your backup yesterday!).

To review all the pros and cons of each type, consult the summary provided in Table 2-1 in the previous chapter. But briefly:

1. Choose Differential if: you mostly use the same files every day, don't care about losing interim versions of your files, and prefer to reuse the same daily backup disks every day.

2. Choose Incremental if: you mostly use different files every day, care about preserving interim versions of your files, and don't mind using lots of floppy disks to keep your backups.

Note: it is possible to preserve interim files with differential backups simply by using a different set of disks each day and rotating them on some schedule (say, every three or five days). But this eliminates one of the key advantages of using a Differential backup: saving on floppy disk use.

### Making Backups of Your Backups

For the sake of security, it is wise to make at least one extra copy of each backup you make and store the copies in a separate place. For instance, many users keep one backup set in the office and take one home. If you have a home-office, perhaps you could keep one with your other disks near the computer, and the other in your safe. Whatever you decide, *do* take the little bit of extra time required to back up your backups!

# PART II

# The FASTBACK PLUS Menu System

This part of Using FASTBACK PLUS contains four chapters. Chapter 4 describes how to use the FASTBACK PLUS menu system to activate procedures, select settings, and use advanced features. It also contains information about how FASTBACK PLUS makes use of the control and function keys on your keyboard, and how to get on-line help while using FASTBACK PLUS.

The remaining chapters in Part II provide illustrated explanations of each activity and option available from the FASTBACK PLUS menu system:

- Chapter 5 covers the Backup menu.
- Chapter 6 covers the Restore menu.
- Chapter 7 covers the Options menu.

In Chapters 5 and 6, the menu selections are arranged according to the order in which the typical user might use them. (The figure on the following page helps to summarize.) This order-of-use arrangement makes it easy for you to see the fundamental steps you will go through when you do basic backup and restore procedures. This arrangement will be particularly helpful to the beginner.

## FASTBACK PLUS *Menu Tree*

|  | **BACK UP** | **RESTORE** | **OPTIONS** |
|---|---|---|---|
| **BEGINNER** | Hard Disk | Hard Disk | User Level |
| | Choose Files | Choose Files | *Beginner* |
| | Destination | Restore Source | *Experienced* |
| | Backup Type | *List of defined floppy drives,* | *Advanced* |
| | *Full* | *plus Regular DOS Drive and* | Installation |
| | *Incremental* | *Path* | *Floppy Drives* |
| | *Differential* | Directory | *Test Hardware* |
| | Preview Backup | *Create Only If Needed* | *Set DMA Speed* |
| | Start Backup | *Use Default* | *Mouse Sensitivity* |
| | *Estimate* | Start Restore | *Quit* |
| | *Start Backup* | *Estimate* | Load Setup File |
| | *Quit* | *Start Restore* | Save Setup File |
| | | *Get History* | |
| | | *Compare Files* | |
| | | *Quit* | |

|  | | | |
|---|---|---|---|
| **EXPERIENCED** | Hard Disk | Hard Disk | User Level |
| | Include Files | Include Files | *Beginner* |
| | Exclude Files | Exclude Files | *Experienced* |
| | Destination | Restore Source | *Advanced* |
| | *List of defined floppy drives,* | *List of defined floppy drives, plus* | Installation |
| | *plus Regular DOS Drive and* | *Regular DOS Drive and Path* | *Floppy Drives* |
| | *Path* | Directory | *Test Hardware* |
| | Backup Type | *Create Only If Needed* | *Set DMA Speed* |
| | *Full* | *Use Default* | *Mouse Sensitivity* |
| | *Incremental* | Write Over | *Quit* |
| | *Differential* | *Never* | History Report |
| | Preview Backup | *Older Files Only* | *View* |
| | Start Backup | *Always* | *Print* |
| | *Estimate* | Start Restore | Old History Reports |
| | *Start Backup* | Estimate | *Delete* |
| | *Quit* | *Start Restore* | *Save* |
| | | *Get History* | Write Verify |
| | | *Compare Files* | *None* |
| | | *Quit* | *Write* |
| | | | *Format/Write* |
| | | | Audible Prompts |
| | | | *Off* |
| | | | *Beep* |
| | | | *Buzzer* |
| | | | *Chime* |
| | | | Overwrite Warning |
| | | | *Off* |
| | | | *Regular Disks* |
| | | | *Backup Disks* |
| | | | *Any Used Disk* |
| | | | Display Colors |
| | | | *Main Menus* |
| | | | *Directory* |
| | | | *Help* |
| | | | *Errors* |
| | | | MS-DOS Command |
| | | | Keystrokes to File |
| | | | Playback Keystrokes |
| | | | Load Setup File |
| | | | Save Setup File |

|  | **BACK UP** | **RESTORE** | **OPTIONS** |
|---|---|---|---|

**ADVANCED**

**BACK UP**
Hard Disk
Include Files
Exclude Files
Files by Date
  *Destination*
  *List of defined floppy*
  *drives, plus Regular*
  *DOS Drive and Path*
  *Backup Type*
  *Full*
  *Incremental*
  *Differential*
  *Preview Backup*
  *Start Backup*
  *Estimate*
  *Start Backup*
  *Quit*

**RESTORE**
Hard Disk
Include Files
Exclude Files
Files by Date
Restore Source
  *List of defined floppy drives, plus*
  *Regular DOS Drive and Path*
Write Over
  *Never*
  *Older Files Only*
  *Always*
Archive Flag
  *Leave Alone*
  *Mark As Not Backed Up*
  *Mark As Backed Up*
User Confirmation
  *Off*
  *Directories Only*
  *Files and Directories*
  *Only on Overwrite*
Directory
  *Create Only If Needed*
  *Use Default*
  *Start Restore*
  *Estimate*
Start Restore
  *Get History*
  *Compare Files*
  *Quit*

**OPTIONS**
User Level
  *Beginner*
  *Experienced*
  *Advanced*
Installation
  *Floppy Drives*
  *Test Hardware*
  *Set DMA Speed*
  *Mouse Sensitivity*
  *Quit*
History Report
  *View*
  *Print*
Old History Reports
  *Delete*
  *Save*
Write Verify
  *None*
  *Write*
  *Format/Write*
Audible Prompts
  *Off*
  *Beep*
  *Buzzer*
  *Chime*
Format Mode
  *Only If Needed*
  *Always Format*
Overwrite Warning
  *Off*
  *Regular Disks*
  *Backup Disks*
  *Any Used Disk*
Compression of Data
  *Off*
  *Save Time*
  *Save Disks*
Display Colors
  *Main Menus*
  *Directory*
  *Help*
  *Errors*
Error Correction
  *On*
  *Off*
Password Protection
Available on Function Keys Only:
MS-DOS Command
Keystrokes to File
Playback Keystrokes
Load Setup File
Save Setup File

Chapter 7, *The Options Menu*, also follows a utilitarian order, although this arrangement is somewhat more arbitrary, since the items on this menu are not required steps in any FASTBACK PLUS procedure. Note also that the Options menu items presented in Chapter 7 are mixed with regard to user level. If you are a beginning computer user, it is probably a good idea to note the user level of an item in this chapter before attempting to use it.

Each menu system chapter begins with its own table of contents, so that you can also use this part of the book as a reference tool while you learn your way around FASTBACK PLUS.

The descriptions of the menu selections provide the following information:

- **Screen illustration**   A "snapshot" showing the menu selection and the choices it offers, if any.
- **Level**   The user level; menu selections with a user level of Beginner apply to all user levels; a designation of Experienced applies to both the Experienced and Advanced levels; and Advanced indicates a menu selection available only at the Advanced level.
- **Purpose**   Tells you what the menu selection does.
- **Action**   Tells you what, if anything, you have to do after you have selected this item from the menu.
- **Default**   Tells you FASTBACK PLUS's default setting for this menu selection.
- **Comments**   Explains any unusual aspects of the menu selection. If no comments are needed, this field does not appear.

# CHAPTER 4

# *Navigating FASTBACK PLUS*

This chapter tells you how to get around and do things in FASTBACK PLUS. It contains instructions for using both the FASTBACK PLUS menus and the function and control keys that FASTBACK PLUS has assigned special operations to.

## Using FASTBACK PLUS Menus

Everything you can do with FASTBACK PLUS you can do by selecting from menus. The FASTBACK PLUS menu system is not large and complex like some programs. On the contrary, the FASTBACK PLUS menu system consists of a main menu (see Figure 4-1) offering three submenus and a Quit option.

Each submenu selection either initiates a straightforward operation (see Figure 4-2), such as choosing files to back up or restore with the Choose Files selection, or presents a short list of choices, such as the three User Levels. Figure 4-3 shows the User Level choice.

*Figure 4-1: The Main Menu*

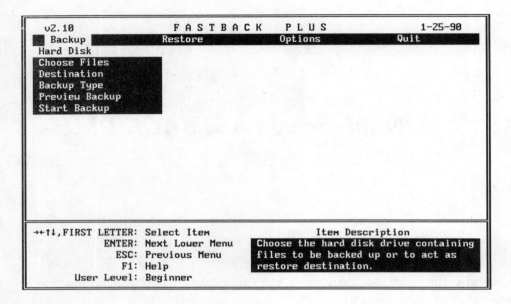

*Figure 4-2: Initiating a FASTBACK PLUS Operation*

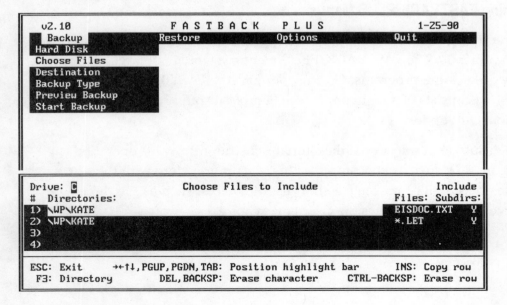

*Figure 4-3: Some Menu Items Present a List of Choices*

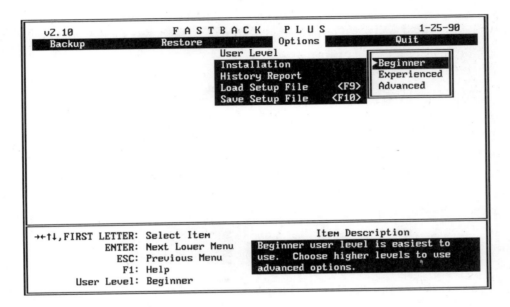

You can select activities and options from FASTBACK PLUS menus in one of two ways:

- Press the first letter of the menu item you want and press ENTER.
- Move the highlight bar with the arrow keys until it is on the item you want, and then press ENTER.

The following keystrokes are all you need to move the highlight bar around, select menu items, and return to previous menus:

- **Arrow keys** The Arrow keys are almost always delegated to cursor movement in popular PC programs. In FASTBACK PLUS, you can use your Up and Down arrow keys to move the highlight bar up and down within a menu, and your Right and Left arrow keys to move back and forth between menus.

- **ENTER**  When you are ready to make a menu selection, move the highlight bar onto the desired item and press ENTER.
- **ESC**  When you are ready to leave a particular menu or level, press ESC (or, in some cases, select the Quit option) to return to the previous menu or level.

Many of the menu selections you make as you use FASTBACK PLUS actually represent *settings* that tell FASTBACK PLUS how to behave when it comes time to back up or restore your files. Once you have selected a particular setting, it stays in effect until you come back and reset it. It is important to understand this because FASTBACK PLUS allows you to save and reuse frequently-needed settings either through the Save/Load Setup Files feature or through the Keystrokes to File/Playback Keystrokes feature. These unique features are described in Chapter 7 and in more detail in Chapters 11 and 12.

## Using Special Keys in FASTBACK PLUS

In addition to the menu system, FASTBACK PLUS makes use of some of the function and control keys on your keyboard for special purposes. The following sections explain how FASTBACK PLUS uses special keys to perform certain tasks.

### Selecting from Menus

The special keys that let you select from menus are:

- **Up Arrow**  Move menu highlight bar to previous item.
- **Down Arrow**  Move menu highlight to next item.
- **Left Arrow**  Move menu highlight bar to previous menu.
- **Right Arrow**  Move menu highlight bar to next menu.
- **ENTER**  Select currently highlighted item on menu.
- **ESC**  Return to previous menu level; or abort current operation.

### Getting On-line Help

Some keys will offer help and information when needed. The following keys will be especially helpful to beginners.

- **F1**  Activates context-sensitive help screens to explain your current situation and options. The higher the user level you choose, the less detailed are the help screens. That is, the Beginner level help screens provide a lot more detail and are geared to beginning computer users. Figure 4-4 shows a Beginner help screen.

*Figure 4-4: A Beginner Help Screen*

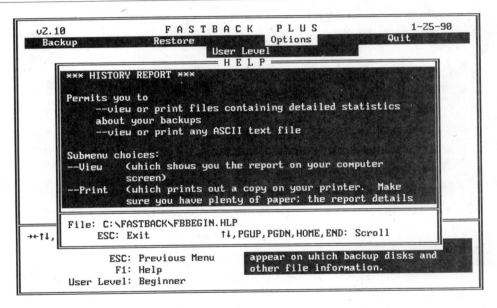

The Advanced level help screens (shown in Figure 4-5) assume a much higher degree of computer knowledge and are therefore less detailed.

The Experienced level help screens fall in between these two extremes.

*Figure 4-5: Advanced Help Screens are Less Detailed*

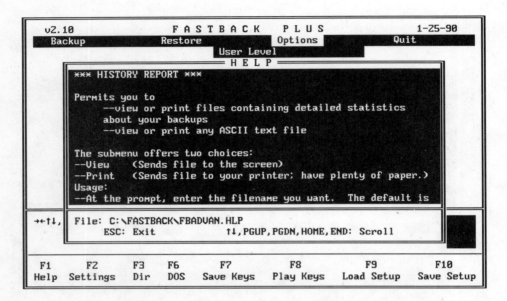

- **F2**  Displays a summary of your current FASTBACK PLUS set-tings. This window is shown in Figure 4-6.

### Selecting Individual Files and Editing the Files List

FASTBACK PLUS offers several keys to help you work with your files:

- **F3**  Creates a context-sensitive, graph-like directory listing called a "Directory Tree" when you are in a situation that calls for you to select files. FASTBACK PLUS builds each directory tree based on the task you are doing. So, for example, if you are selecting files for a backup, F3 displays the directories on the hard disk you have identified; if you are choosing history files for a restore, FASTBACK PLUS constructs a directory tree out of the available history files; and if you are selecting a setup or keystroke file that you have saved, pressing F3 gets you a directory of the .FB files on your disk. Figure 4-7 shows how F3 obtains a directory tree.

*Figure 4-6: F2 Displays Your Current Settings*

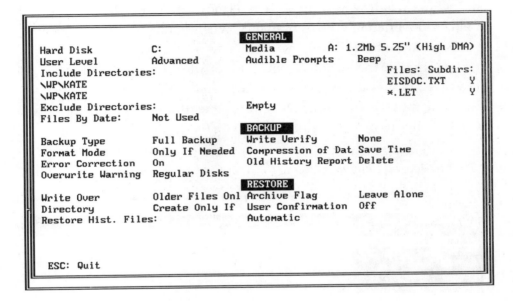

```
                              GENERAL
 Hard Disk          C:       Media          A: 1.2Mb 5.25" <High DMA>
 User Level         Advanced Audible Prompts Beep
 Include Directories:                        Files: Subdirs:
 \WP\KATE                                     EISDOC.TXT    Y
 \WP\KATE                                     *.LET         Y
 Exclude Directories:        Empty
 Files By Date:     Not Used

                              BACKUP
 Backup Type        Full Backup  Write Verify       None
 Format Mode        Only If Needed Compression of Dat Save Time
 Error Correction   On       Old History Report Delete
 Overwrite Warning  Regular Disks

                              RESTORE
 Write Over         Older Files Onl Archive Flag       Leave Alone
 Directory          Create Only If  User Confirmation  Off
 Restore Hist. Files:         Automatic



 ESC: Quit
```

*Figure 4-7: F3 Gets a Directory Tree*

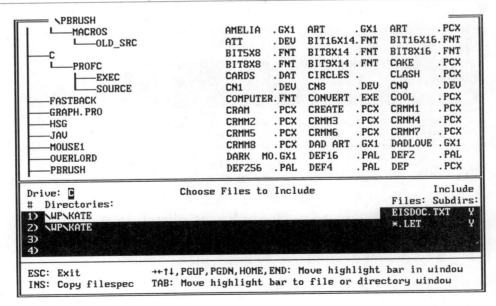

```
       \PBRUSH
        └─MACROS          AMELIA  .GX1  ART    .GX1  ART    .PCX
          └─OLD_SRC       ATT     .DEV  BIT16X14.FNT BIT16X16.FNT
      ─C                  BIT5X8  .FNT  BIT8X14 .FNT  BIT8X16 .FNT
        └─PROFC           BIT8X8  .FNT  BIT9X14 .FNT  CAKE    .PCX
          ├─EXEC          CARDS   .DAT  CIRCLES .     CLASH   .PCX
          └─SOURCE        CN1     .DEV  CN8     .DEV  CNQ     .DEV
     ─FASTBACK            COMPUTER.FNT  CONVERT .EXE  COOL    .PCX
     ─GRAPH.PRO           CRAM    .PCX  CREATE  .PCX  CRMM1   .PCX
     ─HSG                 CRMM2   .PCX  CRMM3   .PCX  CRMM4   .PCX
     ─JAV                 CRMM5   .PCX  CRMM6   .PCX  CRMM7   .PCX
     ─MOUSE1              CRMM8   .PCX  DAD ART .GX1  DADLOVE .GX1
     ─OVERLORD            DARK  MO.GX1  DEF16   .PAL  DEF2    .PAL
     ─PBRUSH              DEF256  .PAL  DEF4    .PAL  DEP     .PCX
─────────────────────────────────────────────────────────────────
 Drive: C          Choose Files to Include              Include
 #  Directories:                             Files: Subdirs:
 1> \WP\KATE                                 EISDOC.TXT    Y
 2> \WP\KATE                                 *.LET         Y
 3>
 4>
─────────────────────────────────────────────────────────────────
 ESC: Exit      →←↑↓,PGUP,PGDN,HOME,END: Move highlight bar in window
 INS: Copy filespec  TAB: Move highlight bar to file or directory window
```

- **TAB**  Jumps to the next field in the window. For example, when you create a list of files to back up or restore in the Choose Files to Include window, you press TAB to move from the **Directories** field to the **Filename** field. Similarly, when you select files to include from a directory tree, you press TAB to move from the directory tree to the accompanying list of files. Figure 4-8 shows how TAB moves the highlight bar to the next active field. In this case, the move is from The Directories: Field to the Files: field in Choose Files to Include Window.

*Figure 4-8: TAB Moves the Highlight Bar to the Next Field*

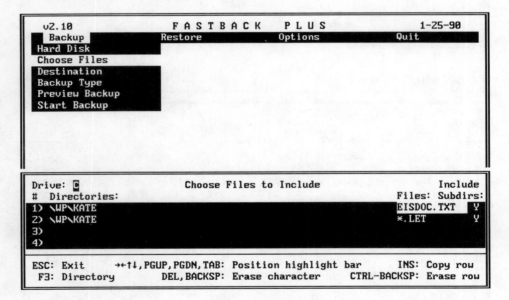

- **Arrow Keys**  Scrolls up and down through either the directory tree or the list of files in the Choose Files to Include window. (Remember that you do *not* use the LEFT and RIGHT ARROW keys to move *across* these screens. Only the TAB key allows you to move horizontally—from field to field—in these windows.)

- **CTRL-BACKSPACE** Deletes any text, such as a default, already in a field. For example, when you select a setup file, FASTBACK PLUS presents the filename of the most recently used setup file as the default selection. If the default filename is not the one you want, you can erase it with CTRL-BACKSPACE. Figure 4-9 shows how you can delete default selections with CTRL-BACKSPACE.

*Figure 4-9: Delete Default Settings With CTRL-BACKSPACE*

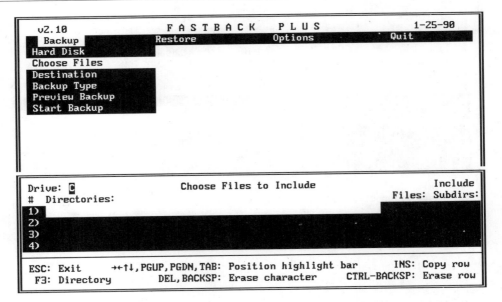

- **INS** Copies the currently highlighted file or directory name into the Choose Files to Include window. Use the INS key to select files and directories from a directory tree. In Figure 4-10 INS copies a pathname from the highlighted file in the directory tree.

### *Activating Certain FASTBACK PLUS Options Without Using the Menu*

The following keys can be used at the Advanced level to activate certain features available on the Experienced level Options menu but not the

Advanced level menu. The keys can also be used at the Beginner and Ex-perienced levels instead of selecting the features from the menu.

*Figure 4-10: INS Copies Pathname from Highlighted Directory*

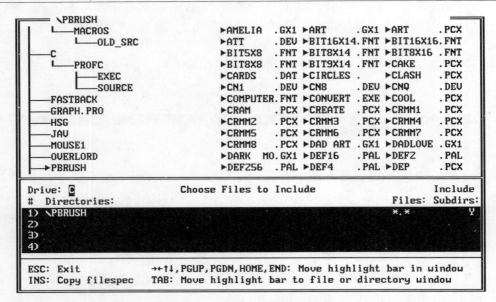

Note: before using the keys described in this section, you may want to see Chapter 7, *The Options Menu*, for full details on the key's associated tasks.

- **F6** Replaces **MS-DOS Command** on the Options menu. Tempo-rarily halts FASTBACK PLUS so that you can issue commands in DOS. (For example, you might want to change your default direc-tory with the DOS CD command before selecting **Use Default Directory** under **Directory** in the Restore menu.) When you are finished in DOS, type EXIT and press ENTER to return to FAST-BACK PLUS. F6 is a convenient way to move between FAST-BACK PLUS and DOS, without having to competely halt FASTBACK PLUS operations.

- **F7**  Replaces **Keystrokes to File** on the Options menu. Prompts for the pathname of the file you want to save your keystrokes in, then records every menu choice and keystroke until you press F7 again, saving the recorded keystrokes in the named file. The file must have an extension of .FB.

- **F8**  Replaces **Playback Keystrokes** on the Options menu. Prompts for the pathname of the file containing the keystrokes to play back, then plays them back exactly as you originally typed them, performing each selected FASTBACK PLUS operation.

- F9  Replaces **Load Setup File** on the Options menu. Prompts for the pathname of the desired setup file, then loads the file and changes the current FASTBACK PLUS settings to reflect those found in the file.

- F10  Replaces **Save Setup File** on the Options menu. Prompts for a pathname, and then saves the current FASTBACK PLUS settings in the indicated file. The file must have an extension of .FB.

# CHAPTER 5

# *The Backup Menu*

This chapter is a complete guide to the Backup menu and all of its features. It is set up for easy reference. Each menu item is shown in a figure and is followed by a descriptive list that shows the menu level, its purpose, any actions you need to take from within the menu, the default setting, and any additional comments or remarks about the item.

The Backup menu shown includes the following:

- Hard Disk
- Destination
- Backup Type
- Choose Files
- Include Files
- Exclude Files
- Files By Date
- Preview Backup
- Start Backup
- Archive Flag

## Hard Disk

**Level:**   Beginner

**Purpose:**   Specify hard disk to back up.

**Action:**   Enter the letter of the drive you want to back up.

**Default(s):**   C: drive

*Figure 5-1: Hard Disk*

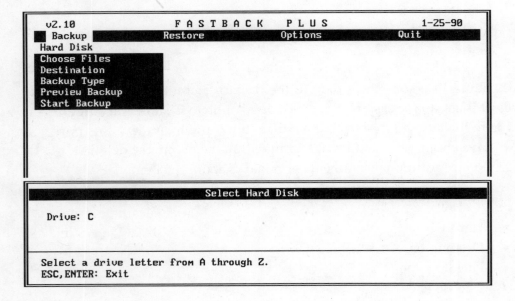

## Destination

**Level**   Beginner

**Purpose:**   Specify floppy drive to send backup files to.

**Action:**   Select from a pop-up list of floppy drives (or other devices) defined at installation.

*Figure 5-2: Destination*

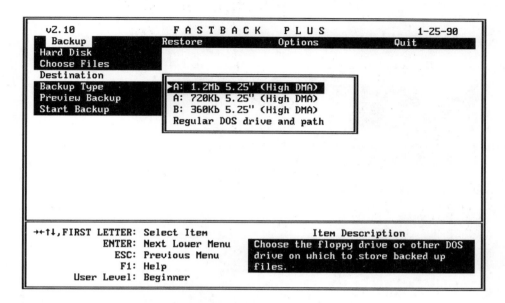

```
 v2.10              F A S T B A C K   P L U S        1-25-90
   Backup          Restore          Options            Quit
 Hard Disk
 Choose Files
 Destination
 Backup Type       ▶A: 1.2Mb 5.25" (High DMA)
 Preview Backup     A: 720Kb 5.25" (High DMA)
 Start Backup       B: 360Kb 5.25" (High DMA)
                    Regular DOS drive and path




 ↔↑↓,FIRST LETTER: Select Item              Item Description
            ENTER: Next Lower Menu    Choose the floppy drive or other DOS
              ESC: Previous Menu      drive on which to store backed up
               F1: Help               files.
       User Level: Beginner
```

**Default(s):** Your A: drive, or both the A: and B: drive if they are the same type.

**Comments:** Any properly installed storage device, such as a tape drive, can be specified here if it was defined during the FASTBACK PLUS installation procedure. Select **Regular DOS drive and path** to specify a device other than your A: or B: floppy drive.

## Backup Type

**Level:** Beginner

**Purpose:** Specify desired backup type.

**Action:** Choose from:

- **Full Backup** Backs up all files on the designated hard disk. (Note: Under Full Backup, you may also select Full Copy, which makes copies of all your files, without creating a history file or marking the files as backed up.)

*Figure 5-3: Backup Type*

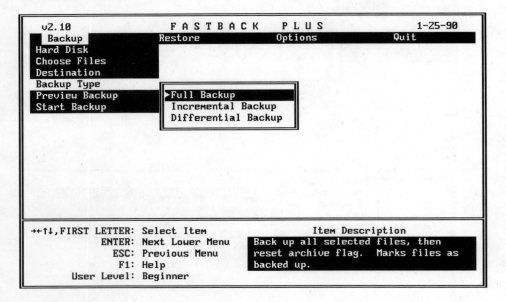

- **Incremental Backup**  Backs up only those files that have changed since the last *incremental* backup, appending the history file to the last full backup's history file. (Note: Under Incremental Backup, you may also select Separate Incremental, which does not append the history file to that of the last full backup.)
- **Differential Backup**  Backs up all files that have changed since the last *full* backup, even if they were backed up in a previous differential backup and have not changed since.

**Default(s):**   Full Backup

**Comments:**   See Chapter 2 for more details on FASTBACK PLUS's backup types.

## Choose Files

**Level:** Beginner

**Purpose:** Select your own files rather than use one of the predefined backup types.

**Action:** Either type pathnames of desired files or directories into the **Choose Files To Include** window, or press F3 to get a Directory Tree and then select files or directories from the tree by highlighting them and pressing INS. Press ESC to save your list of files and return to the Backup menu.

**Default(s):** C:\ *.* Y—tells FASTBACK PLUS to back up all files on your C: drive.

**Comments:** See Chapter 2 for details on methods of file selection.

*Figure 5-4: Choose Files*

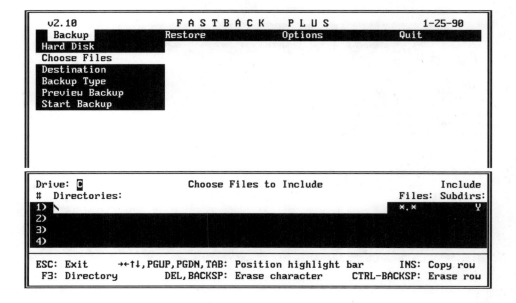

## Include Files

**Level:**   Experienced

**Purpose:**   Select your own files rather than use one of the predefined backup types.

**Action:**   Either type pathnames of desired files or directories into the **Choose Files To Include** window, or press F3 to get a Directory Tree and then select files or directories from the tree by highlighting them and pressing INS. Press ESC to save your list of files and return to the Backup menu.

**Default(s):**   C:\ *.* Y—tells FASTBACK PLUS to back up all files on your C: drive.

**Comments:**   Exactly the same as **Choose Files** on the Beginner Backup menu. See Chapter 2 for details on methods of file selection.

*Figure 5-5: Include Files*

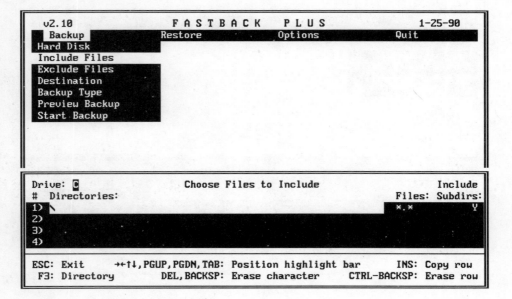

## Exclude Files

**Level:** Experienced

**Purpose:** Explicitly specify files that you want excluded from your Include Files list.

**Action:** Either type path names of files or directories you wish to exclude into the **Choose Files To Exclude** window, or press F3 to get a Directory Tree and then select files or directories from the tree by highlighting them and pressing INS. Press ESC to save your list of files and return to the Backup menu.

**Default(s):** Blank—exclude no files or directories from the Include List.

**Comments:** See Chapter 2 for details on methods of file selection.

*Figure 5-6: Exclude Files*

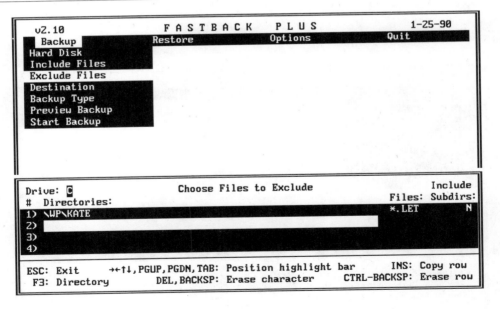

## Files by Date

**Level:**   Advanced

**Purpose:**   Refine your Include List by filtering out files created before or after a period that you specify.

**Action:**   Following the prompts, enter *before* and *after* dates, and then confirm that you want to use the specified dates.

**Default(s):**   *Before* date: 1-1-80
*After* date: 12-31-99
Confirmation: Y

**Comments:**   Do not enter a date prior to 1-1-80, which is the default *before* date. FASTBACK PLUS will interpret any year earlier than '80 to be in the 21st Century, and will therefore exclude every file on your hard disk, causing your backup to fail. See Chapter 2 for more details on using Files by Date.

*Figure 5-7: Files by Date*

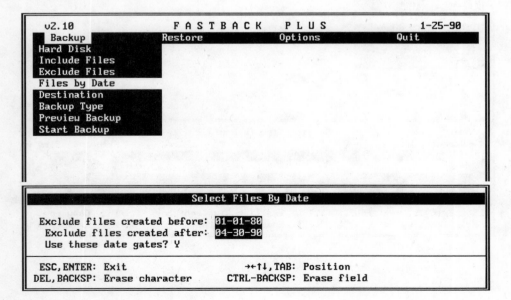

## Preview Backup

**Level:**   Beginner

**Purpose:**   Check the files and directories that either FASTBACK PLUS or you have selected for backup, before actually beginning the backup procedure.

**Action:**   The only action is pressing TAB to switch back and forth as needed between the directories and file windows of the display, which is very similar to the Directory Tree you use when selecting files. When you are satisfied with the selections, press ESC to return to the Backup menu.

**Default(s):**   All files and directories of C:\

**Comments:**   FASTBACK PLUS marks files selected for backup with a small, filled triangle pointing to the filename. Directories and subdirectories that have been selected are also marked in this way.

*Figure 5-8: Preview Backup*

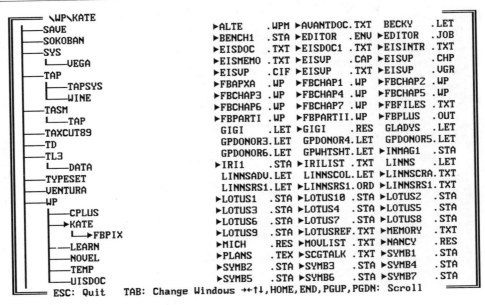

## Start Backup

**Level:**  Beginner

**Purpose:**  Activate the Backup Progress submenu.

**Action:**  Select from:

- **Estimate Disks**  Scans selected files and computes estimated time and number of floppy disks required for the desired backup.
- **Start Backup**  Activates the Backup procedure, displays progress reports on the backup, and prompts you to change floppy disks when necessary.
- **Quit**  Returns you from the Backup Progress screen to the Start Backup menu.

**Default(s):**  No default.

*Figure 5-9: Start Backup*

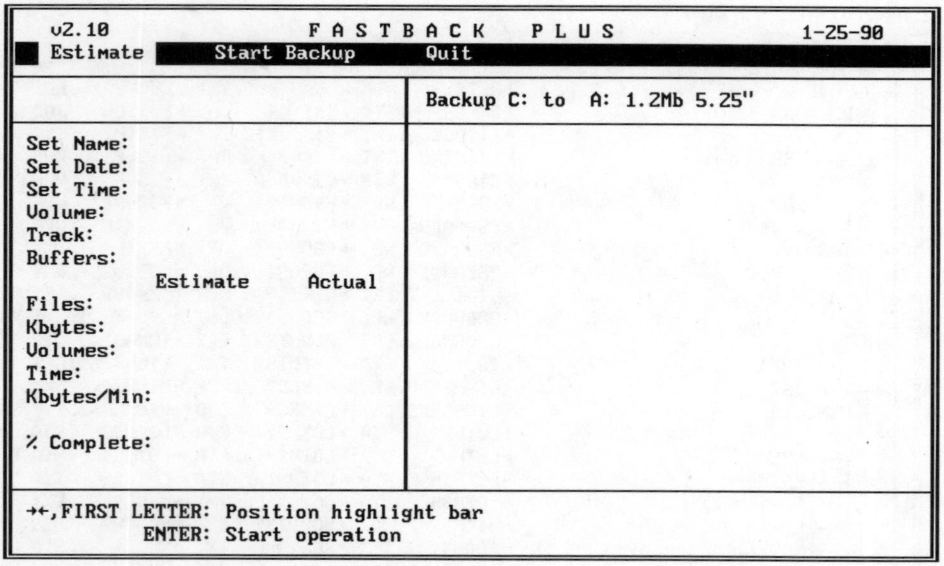

```
 v2.10              F A S T B A C K    P L U S          1-25-90
 ■ Estimate      Start Backup      Quit

                              Backup C: to  A: 1.2Mb 5.25"

 Set Name:
 Set Date:
 Set Time:
 Volume:
 Track:
 Buffers:
              Estimate      Actual
 Files:
 Kbytes:
 Volumes:
 Time:
 Kbytes/Min:

 % Complete:


 →←,FIRST LETTER: Position highlight bar
          ENTER: Start operation
```

**Comments:**   Time and disk estimates are not necessarily accurate. For one thing, they assume no data compression, so if you use one of FASTBACK PLUS's data compression options, you will probably use less time and fewer disks than predicted. Other factors also influence the accuracy of the estimates.

# CHAPTER 6

# *The Restore Menu*

This chapter is a complete guide to the Restore Menu and all of its features. Like Chapter 5, it is set up for easy reference. Each menu item is shown in a figure, followed by a descriptive list that shows the menu level, its purpose, any actions you need to make, the default setting, and other additional comments.

The Restore menu includes the following:

- Restore Source
- Hard Disk
- Choose Files
- Include Files
- Exclude Files
- Files By Date
- Choose History Files
- Write Over
- Archive Flag
- User Confirmation
- Start Restore

## Restore Source

**Level:**   Beginner

**Purpose:**   Specify the floppy drive to restore backup files from.

**Action:**   Select from a pop-up list of floppy drives (or other devices) defined at installation.

**Default(s):**   Your A: drive, or both the A: and B: drive if they are the same
type.

**Comments:**   Any properly installed storage device, such as a tape drive,
can be specified here if it was defined during the FASTBACK PLUS installation procedure. Select Regular DOS drive and path to specify a device other than your A: or B: floppy drive.

*Figure 6-1: Restore Source*

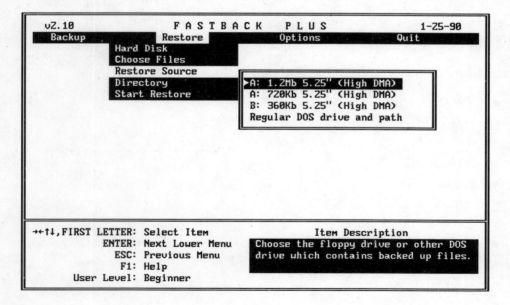

## Hard Disk

**Level:**   Beginner

**Purpose:**   Specify the hard disk to restore backup files to.

**Action:**   Enter the letter of the drive you want.

**Default(s):**   C: drive

*Figure 6-2: Hard Disk*

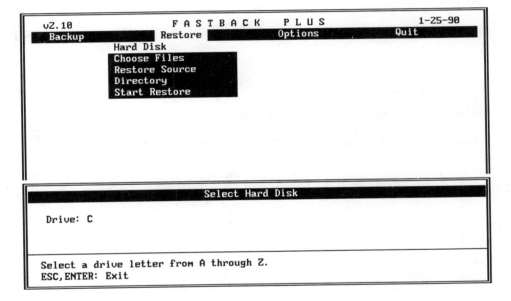

## Choose Files

**Level:**   Beginner

**Purpose:**   Select your own files rather than use one of the predefined backup types.

**Action**   Either type pathnames of desired files or directories into the **Choose Files To Include** window, or press F3 to get a Directory Tree and then select files or directories from the tree by highlighting them and pressing INS. Press ESC to save your list of files and return to the Restore menu.

*Figure 6-3: Choose Files*

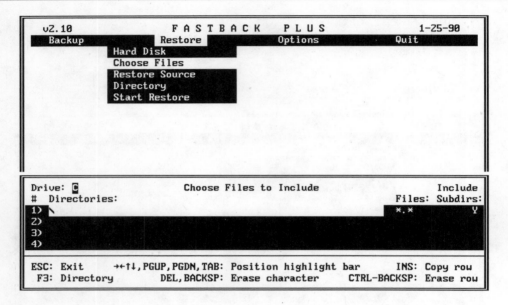

**Default(s):**   C:\ *.* Y—tells FASTBACK PLUS to backup all files on your C drive.

**Comments:**   See Chapter 2 for details on methods of file selection.

## Include Files

**Level:**   Experienced

**Purpose:**   Select the files you want to restore.

**Action:**   Either type pathnames of desired files or directories into the **Choose Files To Include** window, or press F3 to get a Directory Tree and then select files or directories from the tree by highlighting them and pressing INS. Press ESC to save your list of files and return to the Restore menu.

*Figures 6-4: Include Files*

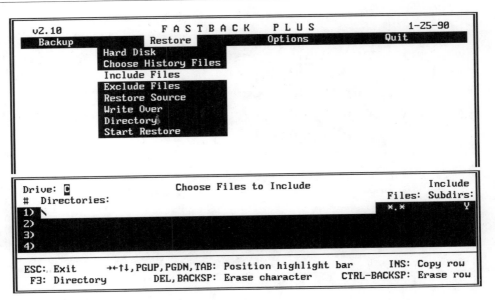

**Default(s):**   C:\ *.* Y—tells FASTBACK PLUS to backup all files on your C: drive.

**Comments:**   Exactly the same as **Choose Files** on the Beginner Restore menu. See Chapter 2 for details on methods of file selection.

## Exclude Files

**Level:**   Experienced

**Purpose:**   Explicitly specify files that you want excluded from your Include Files list.

**Action:**   Either type pathnames of files or directories you wish to exclude into the **Choose Files To Exclude** window, or press F3 to get a Directory

Tree and select files or directories from the tree by highlighting them and pressing INS. Press ESC to your save list of files and return to the Restore menu.

*Figure 6-5: Exclude Files*

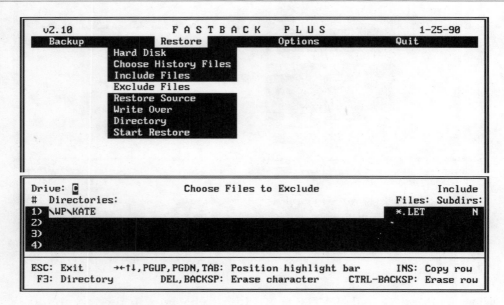

**Default(s):**    Blank—exclude no files or directories from the Include List.

**Comments:**    See Chapter 2 for details on methods of file selection.

## Files by Date

**Level:**   Advanced

**Purpose:**   Refine your Include List by filtering out files created before or after a period that you specify.

**Action:**   Following the prompts, enter *before* and *after* dates, and then confirm that you want to use the specified dates.

*Figure 6-6: Files by Date*

```
 v2.10              F A S T B A C K   P L U S           1-25-90
    Backup          Restore             Options              Quit
                Hard Disk
                Choose History Files
                Include Files
                Exclude Files
                Files by Date
                Restore Source
                Write Over,
                Archive Flag
                User Confirmation
                Directory
                Start Restore


                      Select Files By Date

    Exclude files created before:  01-01-80
     Exclude files created after:  12-31-90
     Use these date gates?  N

    ESC,ENTER:  Exit                    →←↑↓,TAB:  Position
    DEL,BACKSP:  Erase character        CTRL-BACKSP:  Erase field
```

**Default(s):**   *Before* date: 1-1-80
   *After* date: 12-31-99
   Confirmation: Y

**Comments:**   Do not enter a date prior to 1-1-80, which is the default *before* date. FASTBACK PLUS will interpret any year earlier than '80 to be in the 21st Century, and will therefore exclude every file in the backup set, causing your restore to fail.

## Directory

**Level:**   Beginner

**Purpose:**   Tell FASTBACK PLUS whether to:

- Restore your files to their original directories and subdirectories (recreating the original directories if necessary) or

- Restore all specified files to the current default directory on the selected hard disk.

*Figure 6-7: Directory*

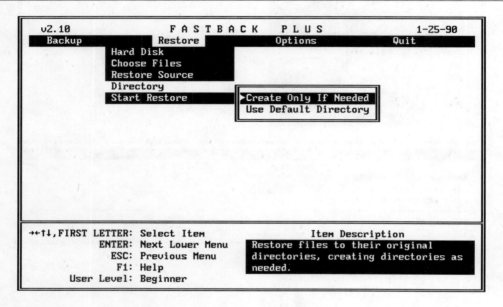

**Action:** Select from:
- **Create Only If Needed** Restore to original directories, re-creating them only if they have been destroyed (for example, if the disk has been reformatted).
- **Use Default Directory** Restore to the current default directory on the destination hard disk. For example, if you are restoring to your C: drive, and the current default directory is the root (that is, the DOS prompt reads: **C:\**), all files will be restored to your root directory.

**Comments:** You can change the default directory on the selected hard disk by pressing F6 to pause FASTBACK PLUS and enter DOS, then using the DOS CD (Change Directory) command. When you have finished in DOS, type EXIT at the DOS prompt and press ENTER to resume your Restore activity in FASTBACK PLUS.

**Default(s):**   Create Only If Needed

## Choose History Files

**Level:**   Experienced

**Purpose:**   Choose whether to:

- Let FASTBACK PLUS restore on the default basis of the most recent Full backup and intervening partial backup history files (a "smart restore"), or
- Select your own set of history files to use for this restore.

*Figure 6-8: Choose History Files*

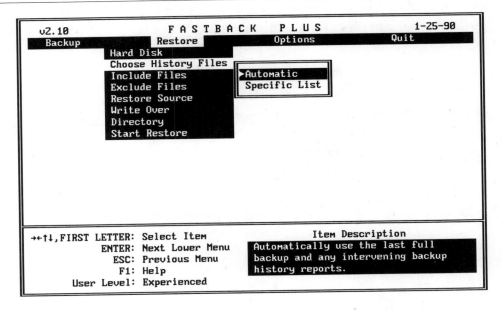

**Action:**   Select from:

- **Specific**  To create a specific list of history files to use for this re-store, you may either: (1) type their pathnames under the screen heading Choose History File for Restore Processing, or (2) press F3 to see a list of available History files and then highlighting the ones you want and press INS to add to the list. Press ESC to your save list of history files and return to the Restore menu.

**Comments:**   Automatic—FASTBACK PLUS uses the most recent history file(s).

**Default(s):**   Automatic.

## Write Over

**Level:**   Experienced

**Purpose:**   Tell FASTBACK PLUS whether to replace existing files on the hard disk with backup files of the same name.

*Figure 6-9: Write Over*

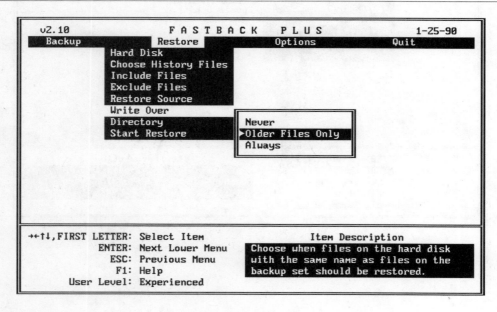

**Action:**   Select from:

- **Never**  Never write over an existing file on the hard disk with a backup file of the same name.
- **Older Files Only**  If the file date of the hard disk is older than the file date of the backup file, write over the hard disk file; otherwise, preserve the hard disk file.
- **Always**  Always write over hard disk files with backup files of the same name, regardless of dates.

**Default(s):**   Older Files Only

## Archive Flag

**Level:**   Advanced

**Purpose:**   Allows you to control whether FASTBACK PLUS marks restored files as backed up or not backed up or simply leaves the archive flag set as it was.

*Figure 6-10: Archive Flag*

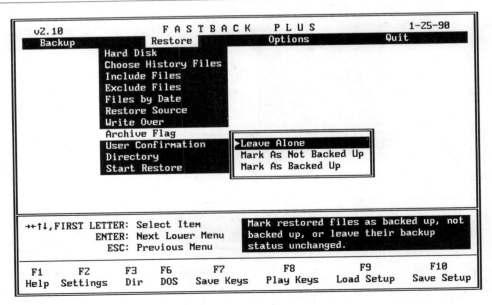

**Action:**   Select from:

- **Leave Alone**  Do not change archive flag settings of restored files.
- **Mark As Not Backed Up**  Mark all restored files as not backed up.
- **Mark As Backed Up**  Mark all restored files as backed up.

**Comments:**   See the section on FASTBACK PLUS Backup Types in Chapter 2 for a discussion of the archive flag.

**Default(s):**   Leave Alone.

## User Confirmation

**Level:**   Advanced

**Purpose:**   Tell FASTBACK PLUS whether to prompt you for confirmation before restoring directories and/or files.

*Figure 6-11: User Confirmation*

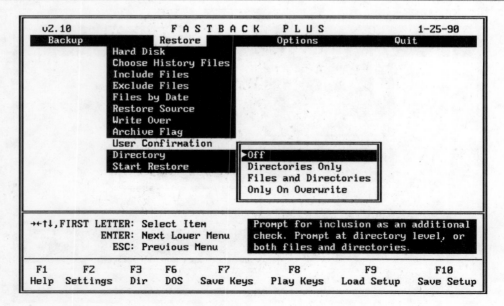

**Action:** Select from:

- **Off** Do not prompt for confirmation at any time.
- **Directories Only** Prompt for confirmation before restoring directories that match the file specifications.
- **Files and Directories** Prompt for confirmation before restoring both files and directories that match specifications.
- **Only on Overwrite** Prompt for confirmation only when about to restore files that will write over files of the same name on the hard disk.

**Comments:** This feature gives you great control over the actual files and directories that FASTBACK PLUS restores, and also gives you the opportunity to avoid accidental overwrites of newer files with older backup versions.

**Default(s):** Off.

## Start Restore

**Level:** Beginner

**Purpose:** Control and monitor the restore process from the Restore Progress menu.

**Action:** Choose from:

- **Estimate** Compare the information in the selected history files to the files on your disk to estimate the number and size of files to be restored, the number of volumes needed, and the names of the required backup sets. Warns if the selected hard disk does not have enough room to restore all the files.
- **Start Restore** Begin the restore process, reporting on restore progress by listing the files as they are restored and various statistics. Prompts you to change floppy disks when needed.

*Figure 6-12: Start Restore Menu*

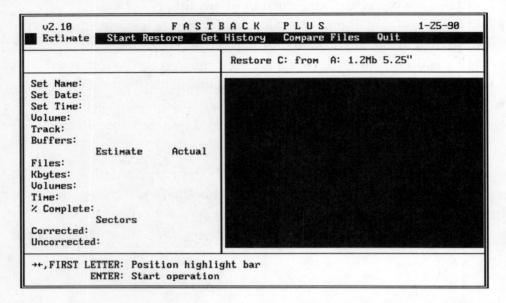

```
 v2.10                F A S T B A C K    P L U S              1-25-90
█ Estimate   Start Restore   Get History   Compare Files   Quit

                                 Restore C: from  A: 1.2Mb 5.25"

 Set Name:
 Set Date:
 Set Time:
 Volume:
 Track:
 Buffers:
            Estimate     Actual
 Files:
 Kbytes:
 Volumes:
 Time:
 % Complete:
            Sectors
 Corrected:
 Uncorrected:

 →←,FIRST LETTER: Position highlight bar
           ENTER: Start operation
```

- **Get History**  Get the history files from your backup set and restore them to the support directory. Use this option if something
  has happened to the history files on your hard disk.

- **Compare Files**  Compare backup files to files on the hard disk.
  Use Compare files before restore if you are planning to reformat
  your hard disk before starting the restore process. This will as-
  sure you that the files you are about to restore are the right files.

- **Quit**  Returns you to the main Restore menu.

**Default(s):**  None.

*Figure 6-13: Get History Selected*

```
 v2.10              F A S T B A C K    P L U S          1-25-90
  Estimate    Start Restore   Get History   Compare Files   Quit

      RESTORING HISTORY          Restore C: from  A: 1.2Mb 5.25"

 Set Name:
 Set Date:   05-09-90
 Set Time:   13:01:28
 Volume:            1
 Track:
 Buffers:    ◆◆◆◆◆◆◆◆
             Estimate    Actual
 Files:          0          0
 Kbytes:         0          0
 Volumes:
 Time:                    0:33
 % Complete:                 0
             Sectors
 Corrected:      0
 Uncorrected     0          Starting history file restore...

 Insert Volume 1 in A:
```

*Figure 6-14: Compare Files Selected*

```
 v2.10              F A S T B A C K    P L U S          1-25-90
  Estimate    Start Restore   Get History   Compare Files   Quit

     PERFORMING COMPARE          Restore C: from  A: 1.2Mb 5.25"

 Set Name:
 Set Date:   05-09-90
 Set Time:   13:48:32
 Volume:            1
 Track:
 Buffers:    ◆◆◆◆◆◆◆◆
             Estimate    Actual
 Files:          0          0
 Kbytes:         0          0
 Volumes:
 Time:                    0:04
 % Complete:                 0
             Sectors
 Corrected:      0
 Uncorrected     0          Starting compare against drive C:...

 Insert Volume 1 in A:
```

# CHAPTER 7

# *The Options Menu*

This chapter is a complete guide to the Options Menu and all of its features. Like Chapters 5 and 6, each menu item is shown in a figure. A descriptive list accompanies each figure, showing the user level, the purpose of the item, any actions you need to take, the default setting, and other additional comments. Options menu includes the following:

- Installation
- User Level
- Save Setup File
- Load Setup File
- Keystrokes to File
- Playback Keystrokes
- MS-DOS Command
- History Report
- Overwrite Disks Warning
- Compression of Data
- Error Correction
- Password Protection
- Write Verify
- Format Mode

- Old History Reports
- Display Colors
- Audible Prompts

The arrangement of the Options menu items in this chapter is somewhat mixed with regard to User Level, so be careful to check the level of each listing before you use that menu selection.

Warning: if you are new to computers, you may want to set the Overwrite Disks Warning to Any Used Disk—even though this Options menu item is at the Experienced level—to ensure that important information will not be overwritten in a backup. Here is the procedure:

- Follow the instructions below to temporarily change the User Level to Experienced.
- Select Overwrite Disks Warning and then select Any Used Disk to change the setting.
- Change the User Level back to Beginner.

## Installation

**Level:**   Beginner

**Purpose:**   Alter your initial installation settings as needed to reflect changes in equipment.

**Action:**   Select from:

- **Floppy Drives**  Set the kind and size of floppy disk drives you have.
- **Test Hardware**  Run a diagnostic test on your computer to determine the data transfer speed your DMA chip will handle.
- **Set DMA Speed**  Set your DMA speed to a *lower* setting. *Never* set the DMA speed to a higher setting than the one determined by the installation hardware test—a higher setting than your

DMA chip can handle could cause serious problems, including data loss.

*Figure 7-1: Installation*

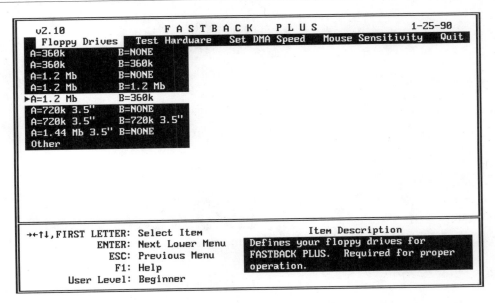

**Mouse Sensitivity**   Adjust the time the cursor takes to respond to mouse movement.

▪ **Quit**  Return you to the Options menu.

**Default(s):**   The defaults for the Installation menu are the settings selected at initial installation of FASTBACK PLUS.

**Comments:**   For more information about installation procedures, floppy drive definitions and hardware testing, see Appendix A.

## User Level

**Level:**   Beginner

**Purpose:**   Change the FASTBACK PLUS user level.

*Figure 7-2: User Level*

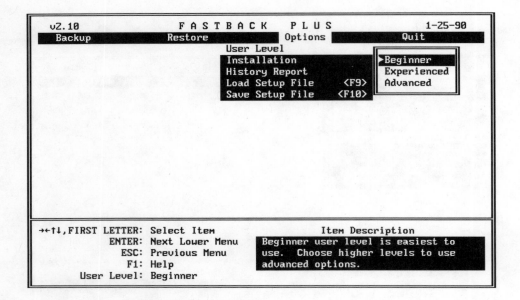

**Action:**   Select from:

- **Beginner**  Allows you to do basic installation, backup and restore procedures, save and use setup files, and examine history files. Offers the most detailed help screens.
- **Experienced**  Supplements Beginner procedures with greater flexibility in file selection, more control of settings and ability to save and use keystroke macros. Help screens are less detailed.
- **Advanced**  Supplements Experienced capabilities with additional file selection filter, and further controls. Help screens assume considerable knowledge of computer.

**Default(s):**   Beginner

**Comments:**   For more details on what activities are available at each User Level, see *Controlling the User Level* in Chapter 2.

*Figure 7-3: Save Setup File*

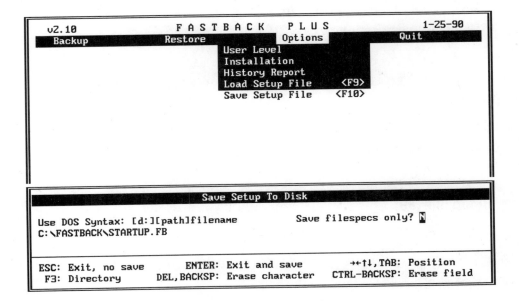

## Save Setup File (F10)

**Level:** Beginner

**Purpose:** Save current FASTBACK PLUS settings to a file for later reuse.

**Action:**

- When FASTBACK PLUS prompts you for a filename to save the current settings under, type a valid DOS pathname specifying the directory, subdirectory (if applicable), and filename you want to use for this setup file. The filename should have an extension of .FB. (Remember—you can press CTRL-BACKSPACE to erase the default.)
- If you want to save *only* your file selections (via Choose Files, Include/Exclude Files and Files by Date), for a particular backup or

restore, press TAB after entering the setup file name to move to the Save filespecs only? field, and change the N to a Y.

- Press ENTER to save the current FASTBACK PLUS settings or your file specifications to the file you named.

**Default(s):**   Your FASTBACK PLUS startup file is offered as a default filename (e.g., C:\FASTBACK\STARTUP.FB), and the default for Save filespecs only is N.

**Comments:**   In addition to selecting Save Setup File from the Options menu, you can activate this feature from anywhere in FASTBACK PLUS by pressing F10.

## Load Setup File (F9)

**Level:**   Beginner

**Purpose:**   Get a previously saved FASTBACK PLUS setup file from your disk so that you can reuse those settings.

*Figure 7-4: Load Setup File*

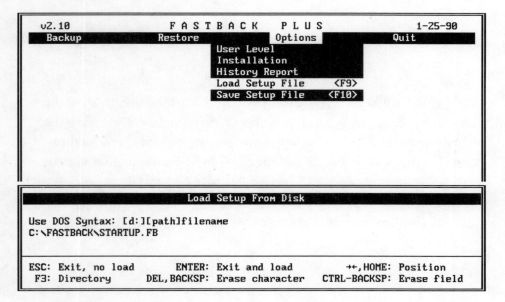

**Action:**   When FASTBACK PLUS prompts you for the name of the setup file to load, type the name and press ENTER. (Remember—you can press CTRL-BACKSPACE to erase the default.) FASTBACK PLUS will change its current settings to match those of the setup file.

Note: if you can't remember the name of the file, you can get a directory listing by pressing F3, then highlight the file you want and press INS. Finally, press ENTER.

**Default(s):**   Your FASTBACK PLUS startup file is offered as a default filename (e.g., C:\FASTBACK\STARTUP.FB).

**Comments:**   In addition to selecting Load Setup File from the Options menu, you can activate this feature from anywhere in FASTBACK PLUS by pressing F9.

## Keystrokes to File (F7)

**Level:**   Experienced

**Purpose:**   Record a sequence of your keystrokes in a file to be played back later.

**Action:**

- When FASTBACK PLUS prompts you for a filename to save your keystrokes under, type a valid DOS pathname specifying the directory, subdirectory (if applicable), and filename you want to use for this keystroke file and press ENTER. (Remember—you can press CTRL-BACKSPACE to erase the default.) As soon as you press ENTER, the cursor returns to the first selection on the FASTBACK PLUS menu.
- Begin making your selections from the FASTBACK PLUS menus. As you do so, every keystroke you make is recorded.

When you are ready to save all your keystrokes in the file you named, either select Keystrokes to File from the Options menu again, or press F7.

*Figure 7-5: Keystrokes to File*

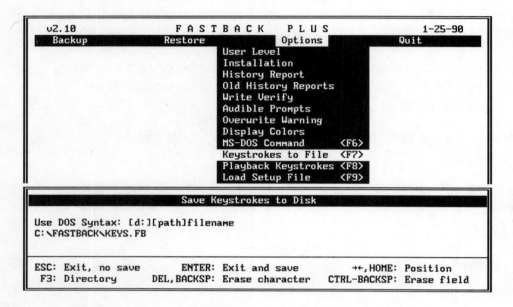

```
v2.10            F A S T B A C K   P L U S        1-25-90
   Backup           Restore        Options           Quit
                              User Level
                              Installation
                              History Report
                              Old History Reports
                              Write Verify
                              Audible Prompts
                              Overwrite Warning
                              Display Colors
                              MS-DOS Command      <F6>
                              Keystrokes to File  <F7>
                              Playback Keystrokes <F8>
                              Load Setup File     <F9>

                       Save Keystrokes to Disk

  Use DOS Syntax: [d:][path]filename
  C:\FASTBACK\KEYS.FB


  ESC: Exit, no save      ENTER: Exit and save     →←,HOME: Position
   F3: Directory     DEL,BACKSP: Erase character  CTRL-BACKSP: Erase field
```

**Default(s):**   FASTBACK PLUS offers a filename of KEYS.FB as the default (e.g., C:\FASTBACK\KEYS.FB).

**Comments:**   FASTBACK PLUS's Keystrokes to File feature is a great time-saver if you want to repeat procedures over and over again. In addition to selecting Keystrokes To File from the Options menu, you can activate this feature from anywhere in FASTBACK PLUS by pressing F7.

## Playback Keystrokes (F8)

**Level:**   Experienced

**Purpose:**   Play back a previously recorded keystroke sequence that you saved in a file.

**Action:**   When FASTBACK PLUS prompts you for the name of the keystroke file to play back, type the name you want and press ENTER. (Remember—you can press CTRL-BACKSPACE to erase the default.)

*Figure 7-6: Playback Keystrokes*

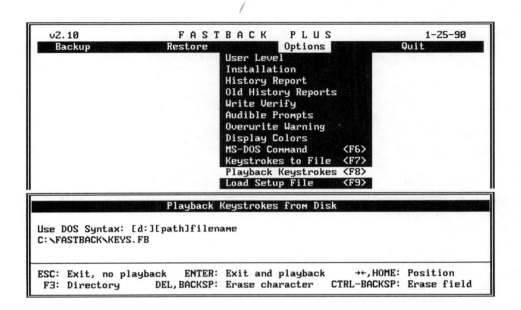

```
 v2.10              F A S T B A C K    P L U S          1-25-90
     Backup              Restore         Options            Quit
                                  User Level
                                  Installation
                                  History Report
                                  Old History Reports
                                  Write Verify
                                  Audible Prompts
                                  Overwrite Warning
                                  Display Colors
                                  MS-DOS Command       <F6>
                                  Keystrokes to File   <F7>
                                  Playback Keystrokes  <F8>
                                  Load Setup File      <F9>

                    Playback Keystrokes from Disk

  Use DOS Syntax: [d:][path]filename
  C:\FASTBACK\KEYS.FB


  ESC: Exit, no playback    ENTER: Exit and playback    →←,HOME: Position
  F3: Directory        DEL,BACKSP: Erase character   CTRL-BACKSP: Erase field
```

FASTBACK PLUS will immediately begin to play back the keystrokes in the file, performing the associated operations, and you will see the screen changing as if you were pressing the keys yourself.

Note: if you can't remember the name of the file, you can get a directory listing by pressing F3, then highlight the file you want and press INS. Finally, press ENTER.

**Default(s):** FASTBACK PLUS offers a filename of KEYS.FB as the default (e.g., C:\FASTBACK\KEYS.FB).

**Comments:** In addition to selecting Playback Keystrokes from the Options menu, you can activate this feature from anywhere in FASTBACK PLUS by pressing F8.

## MS-DOS Command (F6)

**Level:** Experienced

**Purpose:**   Temporarily suspend FASTBACK PLUS to issue one or more commands at the DOS prompt.

**Action:**

- When you see the DOS prompt, enter the desired DOS command(s).
- When you are finished with DOS, type EXIT and then press ENTER to return to FASTBACK PLUS.

**Default(s):**   None.

**Comments:**   In addition to selecting MS-DOS Command from the Options menu, you can activate this feature from anywhere in FASTBACK PLUS by pressing F6.

Note: keep in mind that FASTBACK PLUS will still be resident in memory while you use the MS-DOS Command feature, so you will have less memory available in DOS. If DOS complains of insufficient memory, you

*Figure 7-7: MS-DOS Command*

```
    Calling MS-DOS.  Type "EXIT<Enter>" to return to FASTBACK PLUS.
SPERRY Personal Computer
MS-DOS 3.10 version 1.15
(C)Copyright Microsoft Corp 1981, 1985

Command v. 3.10


The time is  5:44:19.51
Today's date is Thu  5-10-1990

C:\WP\KATE\FBPIX>
```

will have to return to FASTBACK PLUS and select Quit from the Main
menu before entering your DOS commands.

## History Report

**Level:** Beginner

**Purpose:** View or print the history report associated with a particular
backup set.

**Action:**

- Select View or Print from the submenu.
- If the default history file that FASTBACK PLUS offers is not the
  one you want, press CTRL BACKSPACE to clear that name, then
  type the pathname for the desired history file.

*Figure 7-8: History Report*

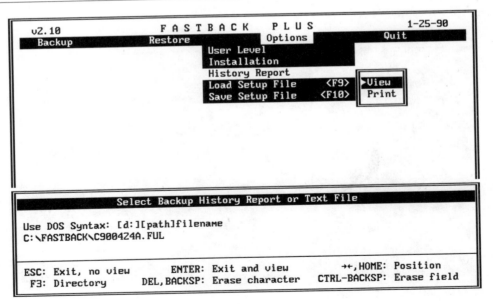

Note: if you can't remember the name of the history file you want, you can get a directory listing by pressing F3, then highlight the file you want and press INS.

**Default(s):**   The default setting for History Report is View. The default filename offered is that of the most recent history report.

**Comments:**   The History Report begins with a description of the backup settings that were used in making this backup, including:

- The hard disk that was backed up
- The name FASTBACK PLUS assigned to the backup set
- The floppy drives that were used as the Destination
- All Include, Exclude, and Files by Date specifications that were used for file selection
- The Archive Flag, Error Correction, and Data Compression settings

*Figure 7-9: An Actual History Report*

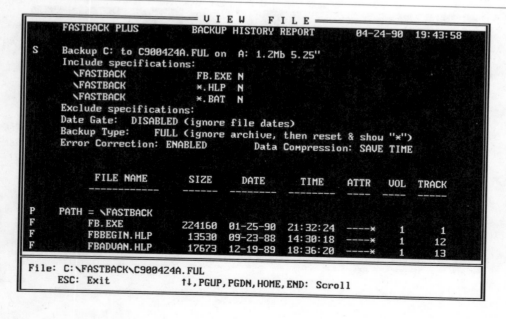

```
====================== V I E W   F I L E =======================
    FASTBACK PLUS              BACKUP HISTORY REPORT        04-24-90  19:43:58

S     Backup C: to C900424A.FUL on  A: 1.2Mb 5.25"
      Include specifications:
         \FASTBACK        FB.EXE  N
         \FASTBACK        *.HLP   N
         \FASTBACK        *.BAT   N
      Exclude specifications:
      Date Gate:   DISABLED (ignore file dates)
      Backup Type:    FULL (ignore archive, then reset & show "*")
      Error Correction: ENABLED        Data Compression: SAVE TIME


              FILE NAME        SIZE      DATE       TIME      ATTR   VOL  TRACK
              ---------        ----      ----       ----      ----   ---  -----

P     PATH = \FASTBACK
F         FB.EXE           224160   01-25-90   21:32:24   ----*    1     1
F         FBBEGIN.HLP       13530   09-23-88   14:30:18   ----*    1    12
F         FBADVAN.HLP       17673   12-19-89   18:36:20   ----*    1    13

 File: C:\FASTBACK\C900424A.FUL
     ESC: Exit              ↑↓,PGUP,PGDN,HOME,END:  Scroll
```

In addition to the FASTBACK PLUS settings used in making the backup, the History Report lists all the files included in the backup. For each file, it tells you:

- The file's name and size in bytes
- The date and time it was created or last modified
- The file's attributes
- The volume and track FASTBACK PLUS recorded it on

## Overwrite Warning

**Level:** Experienced

**Purpose:** Tell FASTBACK PLUS when to warn you that you are about to overwrite existing information on a floppy disk.

**Action:** Select from:

- **Off** Never warn about overwriting.
- **Regular Disks** Warn when about to overwrite a non-backup disk.
- **Backup Disks** Warn when about to overwrite a disk previously used as a FASTBACK PLUS backup disk.
- **Any Used Disk** Warn when about to overwrite any disk containing information.

**Default(s):** Regular Disks

## Compression of Data

**Level:** Advanced

**Purpose:** Set the data compression mode.

**Action:** Select from:

- **Off** Do not use data compression at all.
- **Save Time** Use only idle processor time to do data compression.
- **Save Disks** Do maximum compression, using all time necessary.

*Figure 7-10: Overwrite Warning*

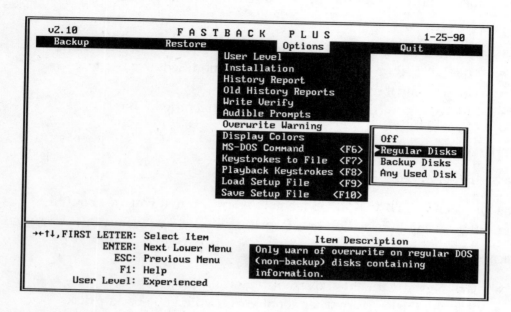

*Figure 7-11: Compression of Data*

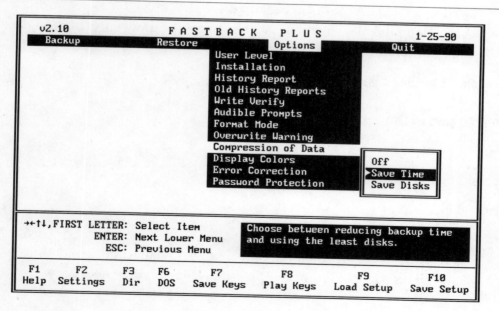

**Default(s):**   Save Time.

**Comments:**   Maximum compression (the Save Disks setting) can be up to 77 percent on some types of files; thus it saves quite a bit of disk space. The Save Time setting, while not achieving maximum compression, can save substantial time and disk space over uncompressed data backup.

## Error Correction

**Level:**   Advanced

**Purpose:**   Turn Advanced Error Correction System on or off.

**Action:**   Select from:

- **On**  Write error correction information to each backup disk so that if the disk is later damaged, FASTBACK PLUS can try to recover missing data.
- **Off**  Do not write error correction information to backup disks.

**Default(s):**   On

**Comments:**   Note that turning error correction off can save some disk space and up to 15 percent of backup time, but it isn't really worth the sacrifice of data security. Depending on the media, FASTBACK PLUS can recover data with up to 13 percent damage to the disk surface.

## Password Protection

**Level:**   Advanced

**Purpose:**   Select a password before making a backup to prevent unauthorized restoration of the backup files.

**Action:**

- Choose your password carefully. It can contain up to 40 characters with no spaces. Warning: you *must* remember your password or you will not be able to restore your backups.

*Figure 7-12: Error Correction*

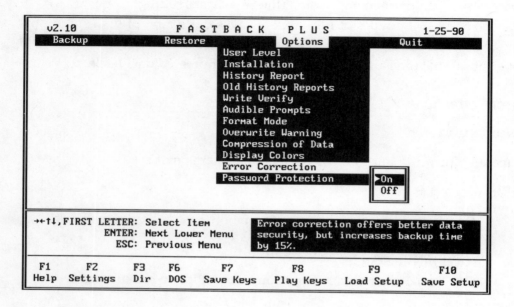

*Figure 7-13: Password Protection*

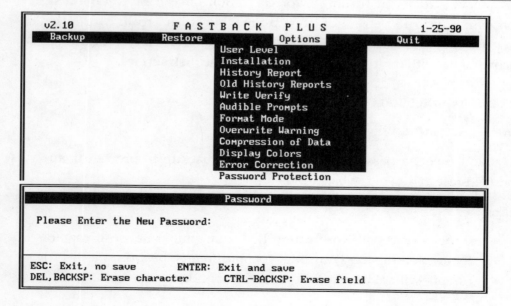

- When prompted, type the password and then press ENTER. You will see the password as you type it, but when your press ENTER, the password will disappear.
- When FASTBACK PLUS prompts for confirmation of the password you just entered, type it in again and press ENTER.

**Default(s):**   None.

**Comments:**   When you want to restore a password-protected backup set, you must first select the Password Protection option from the Options menu, and then enter and confirm the correct password, as you did when you first entered it. If you enter the correct password for the backup set, the restore will proceed without a problem. If, however, you enter an incorrect password or no password at all, FASTBACK PLUS will respond to your restore attempt with a Password Mismatch error. RE-MEMBER—there is no way to restore a password-protected backup without the correct password.

If you make a typing mistake when entering a password prior to restoring your files, you can press SPACE and FASTBACK PLUS will let you try again. If you can't remember the password for the backup set you want, you can press ESC to abort and skip doing the restore until you have remembered the correct password.

## Write Verify

**Level:**   Experienced

**Purpose:**   Tell FASTBACK PLUS whether to verify backed up data against the original data.

**Action:**   Select from:

- **None**  Do not write verify backup data.
- **Write**  Read back every byte of backed up data and compare it to the original byte.
- **Format/Write**  Write verify only when the disk has been formatted.

*Figure 7-14: Write Verify*

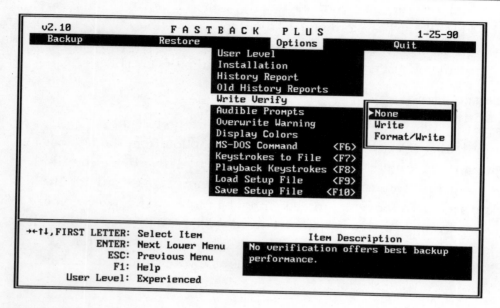

**Default(s):**   None

**Comments:**   Using Write Verify can double your backup time.

## Format Mode

**Level:**   Advanced

**Purpose:**   Tell FASTBACK PLUS when to format backup disks.

**Action:**   Select from:

- **Only If Needed**  Do not bother to reformat a formatted disk.
- **Always Format**  Always format backup disks.

**Default(s):**   Only If Needed.

*Figure 7-15: Format Mode*

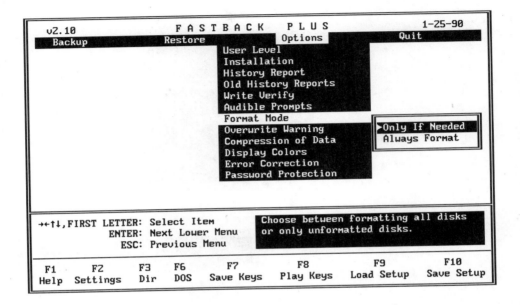

### Old History Reports

**Level:**   Experienced

**Purpose:**   Tell FASTBACK PLUS whether to Save or Delete history reports from previous backups.

**Action:**   Select from:

- **Save**  Keep old history files on disk.
- **Delete**  After a new full backup, delete history reports from the previous full and partial backups.

**Default(s):**   Delete.

### Display Colors

**Level:**   Experienced

*Figure 7-16: Old History Reports*

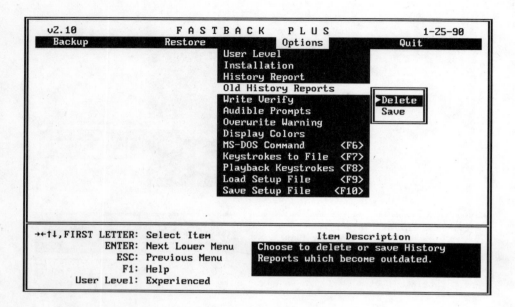

**Purpose:**   Customize FASTBACK PLUS screen colors.

**Action:**

- Select from a submenu of screen types to change: Main Menus, Directories, Help, and Errors. A menu of items whose color you can change on the chosen screen type appears, listing the current colors and the possibilities for change.
- Change the color of the highlighted selection by holding down the SHIFT key and pressing the UP ARROW or DOWN ARROW until the color you want appears in the "SAMPLE" box to the right of the colors screen.

**Default(s):**   Whatever colors were in effect when you installed FAST-BACK PLUS.

*Figure 7-17: Display Colors*

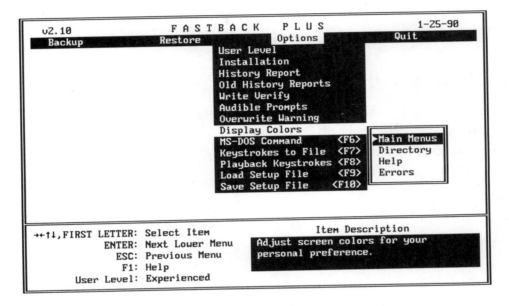

*Figure 7-18: Main Menu Colors Screen*

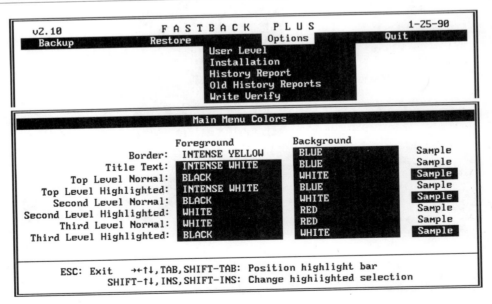

## Audible Prompts

**Level:**   Experienced

**Purpose:**   Turn on or off the beep that accompanies the screen reminder to change disks.

**Action:**   Select from:

- **Off**  Do not give audible prompt with disk change reminder.
- **Beep**  Use beep as audible prompt.
- **Buzzer**  Use buzzer as audible prompt.
- **Chime**  Use chime as audible prompt.

**Default(s):**   Beep. You will hear a "beep" sound when it is time to change disks, unless you turn this feature off or change the setting.

*Figure 7-19: Audible Prompts*

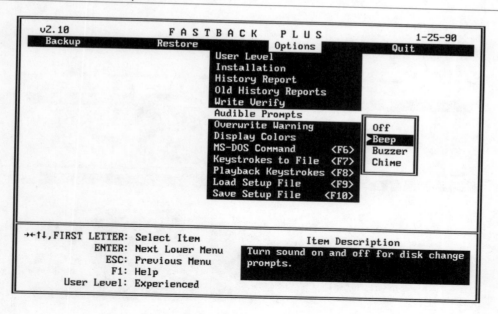

# PART III

# FASTBACK PLUS Tutorials

Chapters 8 through 11 contain illustrated, step-by-step tutorials that "walk" you through the most common FASTBACK PLUS backup and restore procedures.

- Chapter 8 guides you through the steps for both a full backup and a full restore of your hard disk, making use of FASTBACK PLUS's default settings.
- Chapter 9 shows you how to do automatic partial backups—only files that have changed since your last full or incremental backup—using the **Backup Type** setting.
- Chapter 10 demonstrates how to back up and restore only those individual files and directories that you hand-select, using the **Choose Files, Include Files, Exclude Files** and **Files by Date** features. This chapter also shows you how to save the resulting list of files in a FASTBACK PLUS *setup file*.
- Chapter 11 offers a short tutorial on recording and playing back keystrokes with FASTBACK PLUS's **Keystrokes to File** and **Playback Keystrokes** features.

Each procedure is described in easy, single steps, showing you how to select the proper settings for the desired task. A figure accompanies each procedure and shows approximately what your computer screen should look like at each step. Of course, not every screen illustration will look exactly like yours, since you have your own, unique set of files. But you should be able to tell from the illustrations if you have made a mistake or FASTBACK PLUS is not behaving in the expected way.

Once you have completed the tutorials in these chapters, you will be familiar enough with FASTBACK PLUS's features and operating procedures to design your own backup and restore routines and begin using FASTBACK PLUS regularly on your own.

Important: if you have not already installed FASTBACK PLUS on your computer, stop and do so now. You will find complete installation instructions in Appendix A: *Installing FASTBACK PLUS.*

*CHAPTER 8*

# *Tutorials: Full Backup/Full Restore*

## Making a Full Backup

**Step 1**   If you have not already started up FASTBACK PLUS, do so now by typing FB and pressing ENTER at your DOS command prompt:

```
C:>FB
```

When you start up FASTBACK PLUS, you are automatically installing a whole set of FASTBACK PLUS menu settings as well. These are called the *default settings*. FASTBACK PLUS's default settings are designed to make a full backup of your C: hard disk drive, including all directories and subdirectories and the files they contain, from the root directory down to the last file.

Before we get started making a full backup of your hard disk, we can take a look at the default settings.

**Step 2**   To examine your current FASTBACK PLUS settings, press F2.

FASTBACK PLUS displays a screen showing all your current settings. Figure 8-1 shows FASTBACK PLUS's default settings.

*Figure 8-1: Press F2 to See Your Current Settings*

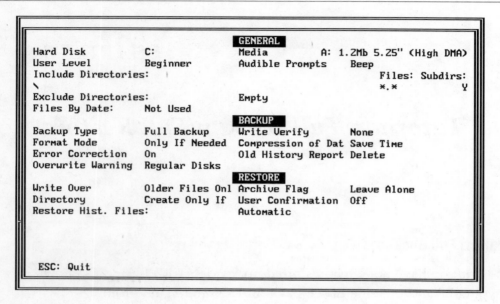

```
                              GENERAL
   Hard Disk        C:        Media        A: 1.2Mb 5.25" (High DMA)
   User Level       Beginner  Audible Prompts  Beep
   Include Directories:                        Files: Subdirs:
   \                                           *.*         Y
   Exclude Directories:        Empty
   Files By Date:   Not Used
                              BACKUP
   Backup Type      Full Backup   Write Verify    None
   Format Mode      Only If Needed Compression of Dat Save Time
   Error Correction On            Old History Report Delete
   Overwrite Warning Regular Disks
                              RESTORE
   Write Over       Older Files Onl Archive Flag    Leave Alone
   Directory        Create Only If User Confirmation Off
   Restore Hist. Files:          Automatic



   ESC: Quit
```

As you can see, FASTBACK PLUS is set up to make a full backup (Backup Type: Full) of your C: drive (Hard Disk: C:), including every file on the disk (\        *.* Y).

**Step 3**  Press ESC to return to the FASTBACK PLUS Main menu.

**Step 4**  Select **Start Backup** from the Backup menu.

To select an item from any FASTBACK PLUS menu, either use the ARROW keys to move the highlight bar to the item you wish to select, or press the first letter of the desired item to jump right to it. Then press ENTER to select the highlighted item.

FASTBACK PLUS's "home" position is the first selection on the Backup menu, Hard Disk, so you need only move the highlight bar down to Start Backup. Figure 8-2 shows FASTBACK PLUS's home position on the Backup menu.

*Figure 8-2: The Home Position*

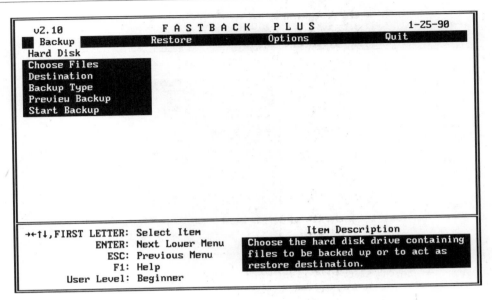

When you select Start Backup, the screen changes to the Backup Progress menu. Near the top of this screen, you see three selections: Estimate, Start Backup and Quit. Figure 8-3 shows the Backup Progress menu.

You have the choice of starting your backup immediately, or using the **Estimate** feature to first get an estimate of the time and number of disks that will be required to complete the backup. Also, using Estimate is necessary if you want FASTBACK PLUS to report on its progress during the backup.

We are going to take advantage of the Estimate feature before beginning our sample backup procedure, to show you how it will prevent you from being caught short of time or disks.

**Step 5**   Select Estimate from the Backup Progress menu.

*Figure 8-3: The Backup Progress Menu*

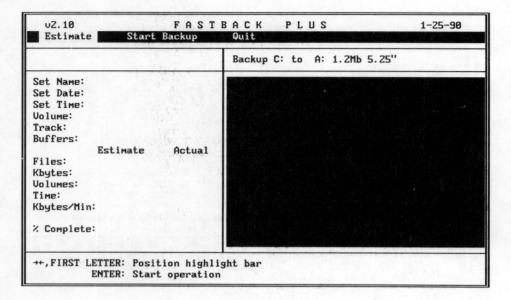

FASTBACK PLUS will begin to scan your hard disk to determine the number and size of the files to be backed up—you will see the filenames scroll by on the right side of the screen during the scanning process. When FASTBACK PLUS has scanned the entire disk, an estimate of the job will appear on the left side of the screen. Figure 8-4 shows what your screen will look like when displaying the estimate.

In the bottom, left-hand quarter of the screen, FASTBACK PLUS presents the following estimated information:

- **Files:**  The number of files on your hard disk.
- **Kbytes:**  The total size of all the files, in kilobytes.
- **Volumes:**  The estimated number of floppy disks (volumes) required to complete this backup. Note that the actual number of floppies required for your later backups will depend on the data

compression setting you use—the highest compression setting, Save Disks, requires the fewest disks.

- **Time:** The estimated time it will take to complete this backup, given in MINUTES:SECONDS. For example, 16:20 indicates that the backup will take approximately 16 minutes and 20 seconds.

- **Kbytes/Min:** The speed FASTBACK PLUS will use to make this backup, given in kilobytes per minute. Again, the speed will vary according to the data compression setting you use. The default data compression setting, Save Time, uses only idle processor time for data compression, and thus FASTBACK PLUS will report a higher backup speed than if you set data compression to Save Disks.

Note: after seeing FASTBACK PLUS's estimate of the time and disks required for this tutorial backup, if you think you won't have enough time or disks, you can select Quit from the Backup Progress menu to return to the Main menu.

*Figure 8-4: FASTBACK PLUS Estimates Required Time and Disks*

```
 v2.10              F A S T B A C K    P L U S          1-25-90
 Estimate       Start Backup        Quit

                                    Backup C: to  A: 1.2Mb 5.25"

 Set Name:                          \WP\NOVEL\
 Set Date:   05-14-90               \WP\WISDOC\
 Set Time:   12:09:46               \WP\TEMP\
 Volume:                            \HSG\
 Track:                             \ASMDISK\
 Buffers:                           \ASMDISK\SCREEN\
             Estimate    Actual     \ASMDISK\SHOW\
 Files:         2146        0       \PUR\
 Kbytes:       29067        0       \SOKOBAN\
 Volumes:         27                \GRAPH.PRO\        .
 Time:         16:20      0:24      \JAV\
 Kbytes/Min:    1779        0       \BLUEDISK\
                                    \TAXCUT89\
 % Complete:                 0      ...Backup estimate completed.
                                    (Data compression may reduce this time.)

 +←,FIRST LETTER: Position highlight bar
            ENTER: Start operation
```

If you wish to leave FASTBACK PLUS for now, select Quit from the Main menu also.

**Step 6**   As an added precaution, check your floppy disk drives now to make sure you have not left a disk in them. Any disk in the backup drive when you begin the backup will be overwritten!

**Step 7**   Select **Start Backup** from the Backup Progress menu (see Figure 8-5).

You will immediately see the message **PERFORMING BACKUP** on the left, just below the menu bar at the top of the Backup Progress menu. This is shown in Figure 8-6.

The first thing FASTBACK PLUS does when you begin a backup is assign the backup set a name and note the date and time you started the backup. You will see these appear in the progress screen. Figure 8-7 illustrates the anatomy of a Backup Set Name.

*Figure 8-5: Select Start Backup to Begin the Backup Process*

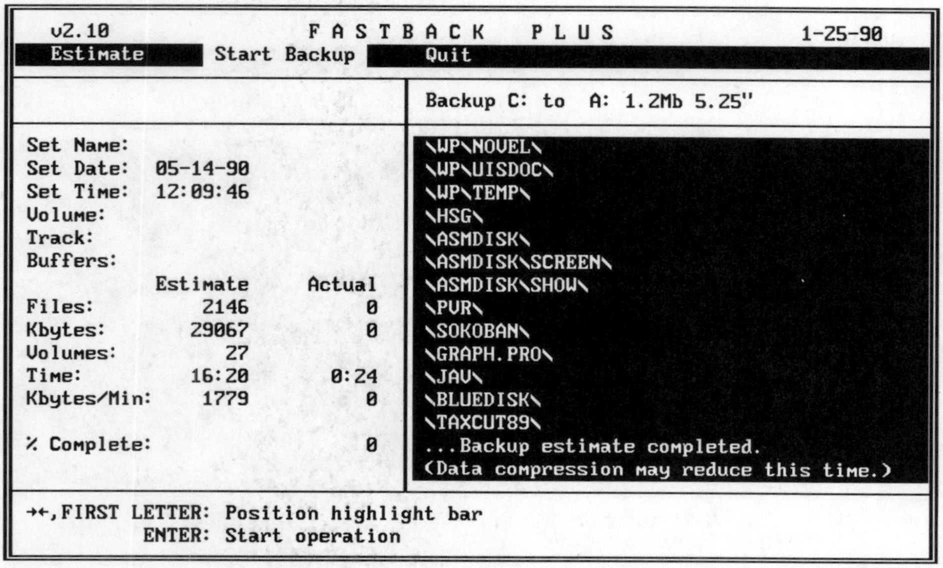

```
  v2.10                F A S T B A C K    P L U S          1-25-90
   Estimate      Start Backup        Quit

                                  Backup C: to  A: 1.2Mb 5.25"

 Set Name:                        \WP\NOVEL\
 Set Date:    05-14-90            \WP\UISDOC\
 Set Time:    12:09:46            \WP\TEMP\
 Volume:                          \HSG\
 Track:                           \ASMDISK\
 Buffers:                         \ASMDISK\SCREEN\
              Estimate    Actual  \ASMDISK\SHOW\
 Files:         2146          0   \PUR\
 Kbytes:       29067          0   \SOKOBAN\
 Volumes:         27              \GRAPH.PRO\
 Time:         16:20       0:24   \JAV\
 Kbytes/Min:    1779          0   \BLUEDISK\
                                  \TAXCUT89\
 % Complete:                  0   ...Backup estimate completed.
                                  (Data compression may reduce this time.)

 →←,FIRST LETTER: Position highlight bar
           ENTER: Start operation
```

*Figure 8-6: FASTBACK PLUS Begins to Back Up Your Files*

```
┌─────────────────────────────────────────────────────────────────┐
│  v2.10              F A S T B A C K   P L U S        1-25-90      │
│  ▐Estimate▌    Start Backup    ▐Quit▌                             │
├─────────────────────────────────┬─────────────────────────────────┤
│   ▐ PERFORMING BACKUP ▌         │ Backup C: to  A: 1.2Mb 5.25"    │
│                                 │                                 │
│  Set Name:  C900514A            │ \HSG\                           │
│  Set Date:  05-14-90            │ \ASMDISK\                       │
│  Set Time:  12:13:56            │ \ASMDISK\SCREEN\                │
│  Volume:          1             │ \ASMDISK\SHOW\                  │
│  Track:                         │ \PUR\                           │
│  Buffers:   ◆◆◆◆◆◆◆◆            │ \SOKOBAN\                       │
│             Estimate   Actual   │ \GRAPH.PRO\                     │
│  Files:        2146        11   │ \JAV\                           │
│  Kbytes:      29067       128   │ \BLUEDISK\                      │
│  Volumes:        27         1   │ \TAXCUT89\                      │
│  Time:        16:20      0:11   │ ...Backup estimate completed.   │
│  Kbytes/Min:   1779       698   │ (Data compression may reduce this time.) │
│                                 │                                 │
│  % Complete:                0   │ Starting backup of C: on volume 1... │
│                                 │ \DM.EXE                         │
├─────────────────────────────────┴─────────────────────────────────┤
│  Insert Volume 1 in A:                                            │
└─────────────────────────────────────────────────────────────────┘
```

*Figure 8-7: Anatomy of a Backup Set Name*

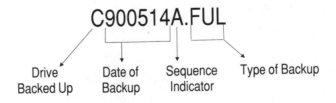

FASTBACK PLUS creates very straightforward names for your backup sets. They consist of the letter of the backed-up hard disk, followed by the date the backup was made (in the YYMMDD format), followed by a *Sequence Indicator*—a letter indicating whether it was the first backup of the day (**A**), the second (**B**), the third (**C**), and so on. FASTBACK PLUS will later create a *history file* for the backup, (which lists the files and gives statistics about them) using the set name with a file extension that indicates what type of backup it is.

**Step 8**   Follow FASTBACK PLUS's prompts for inserting and removing floppy disks as each one gets filled up with your backed up files.

The initial prompt reads:

**Insert Volume 1 in Drive A:**

Note: you do not need to use the DOS FORMAT command on the disks before using them in your backup. FASTBACK PLUS automatically formats any floppy disk that needs formatting, before writing your files to it.

At the sound of the beep, you will be prompted to insert Volume 2, Volume 3, and so on, each time FASTBACK PLUS is ready for you to insert a new floppy disk.

**Step 9**   As you remove each filled floppy disk from the drive, label it with the correct Set Name and Volume number from the screen.

As a general rule, it is very important to label your backup disks as soon as they come out of the drive. Otherwise, you will have a very confusing time, with a lot of disk switching, when you try to restore your backed up files.

As your backup proceeds, the backed up files scroll by on the right side of the screen. At the same time, FASTBACK PLUS reports its progress on the left side of the screen, by filling in the Actual column with figures you can compare to the estimated figures you received earlier. Note the % Complete: indicator, which is constantly updated to let you know how close FASTBACK PLUS is to finishing the backup. This is shown in Figure 8-8.

*Figure 8-8: Percent Completed Shown at Bottom of Screen*

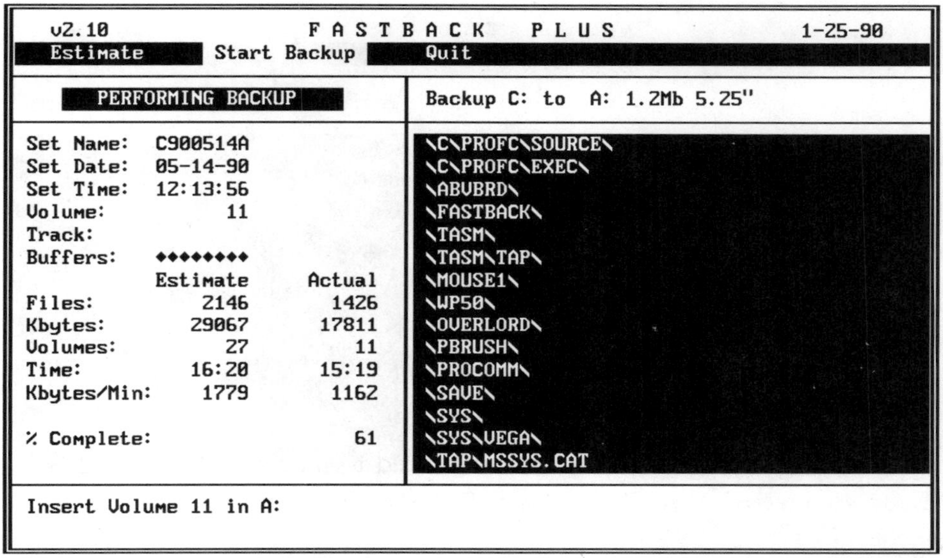

```
  v2.10              F A S T B A C K   P L U S        1-25-90
 ┌──────────┐
 │ Estimate │    Start Backup      Quit
 └──────────┘
 ┌─────────────────────────────────┬─────────────────────────────────┐
 │  ┌──────────────────────────┐   │  Backup C: to  A: 1.2Mb 5.25"   │
 │  │   PERFORMING BACKUP      │   │                                 │
 │  └──────────────────────────┘   │                                 │
 │  Set Name:  C900514A            │  \C\PROFC\SOURCE\               │
 │  Set Date:  05-14-90            │  \C\PROFC\EXEC\                 │
 │  Set Time:  12:13:56            │  \ABVBRD\                       │
 │  Volume:          11            │  \FASTBACK\                     │
 │  Track:                         │  \TASM\                         │
 │  Buffers:   ◆◆◆◆◆◆◆◆            │  \TASM\TAP\                     │
 │             Estimate   Actual   │  \MOUSE1\                       │
 │  Files:         2146     1426   │  \WP50\                         │
 │  Kbytes:       29067    17811   │  \OVERLORD\                     │
 │  Volumes:         27       11   │  \PBRUSH\                       │
 │  Time:        16:20    15:19    │  \PROCOMM\                      │
 │  Kbytes/Min:   1779     1162    │  \SAVE\                         │
 │                                 │  \SYS\                          │
 │  % Complete:             61     │  \SYS\VEGA\                     │
 │                                 │  \TAP\MSSYS.CAT                 │
 ├─────────────────────────────────┴─────────────────────────────────┤
 │  Insert Volume 11 in A:                                            │
 └────────────────────────────────────────────────────────────────────┘
```

Don't be alarmed if the final Actual figures do not exactly match the estimated figures. After all, an estimate is only an estimate, and several factors, such as compression performance, using unformatted disks, and the speed with which you switch disks during the backup, can influence the actual speed of your backup.

**Step 10**   When your backup is complete, select **Quit** from the Backup Progress menu to return to the Main FASTBACK PLUS menu. Figure 8-9 shows this procedure.

If you want to leave FASTBACK PLUS for now, select Quit from the Main menu as well. This is shown in Figure 8-10.

## Restoring Your Full Backup

Restoring your most recent full backup can be a life-saver if accident, theft or damage has wiped out all or part of your hard disk.

*Figure 8-9: The Backup is Completed*

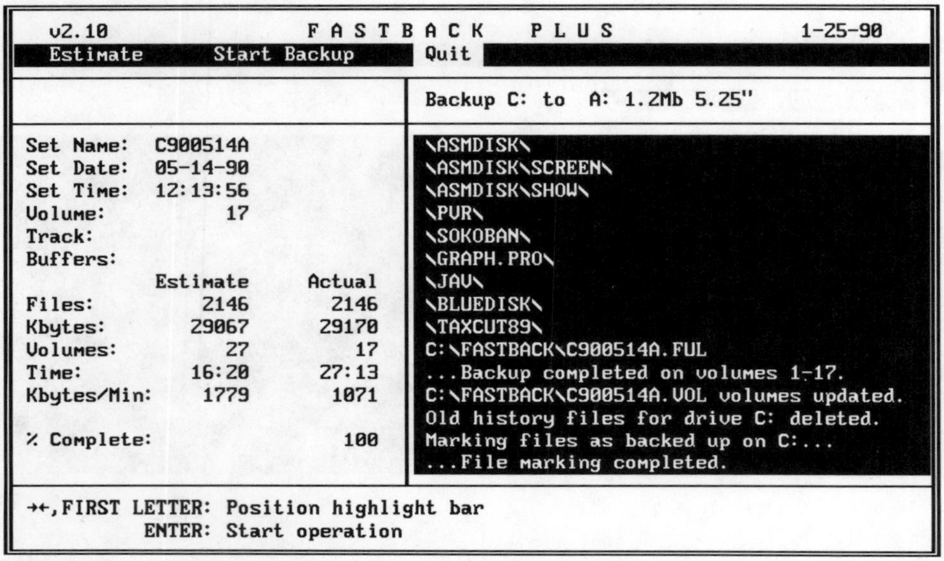

```
 v2.10               F A S T B A C K   P L U S          1-25-90
  Estimate        Start Backup      Quit

                                 Backup C: to  A: 1.2Mb 5.25"

 Set Name:  C900514A              \ASMDISK\
 Set Date:  05-14-90              \ASMDISK\SCREEN\
 Set Time:  12:13:56              \ASMDISK\SHOW\
 Volume:          17              \PUR\
 Track:                           \SOKOBAN\
 Buffers:                         \GRAPH.PRO\
             Estimate    Actual   \JAU\
 Files:          2146      2146   \BLUEDISK\
 Kbytes:        29067     29170   \TAXCUT89\
 Volumes:          27        17   C:\FASTBACK\C900514A.FUL
 Time:          16:20     27:13   ...Backup completed on volumes 1-17.
 Kbytes/Min:     1779      1071   C:\FASTBACK\C900514A.VOL volumes updated.
                                  Old history files for drive C: deleted.
 % Complete:                100   Marking files as backed up on C:...
                                  ...File marking completed.

 →←,FIRST LETTER: Position highlight bar
           ENTER: Start operation
```

*Figure 8-10: Select Quit to Leave FASTBACK PLUS*

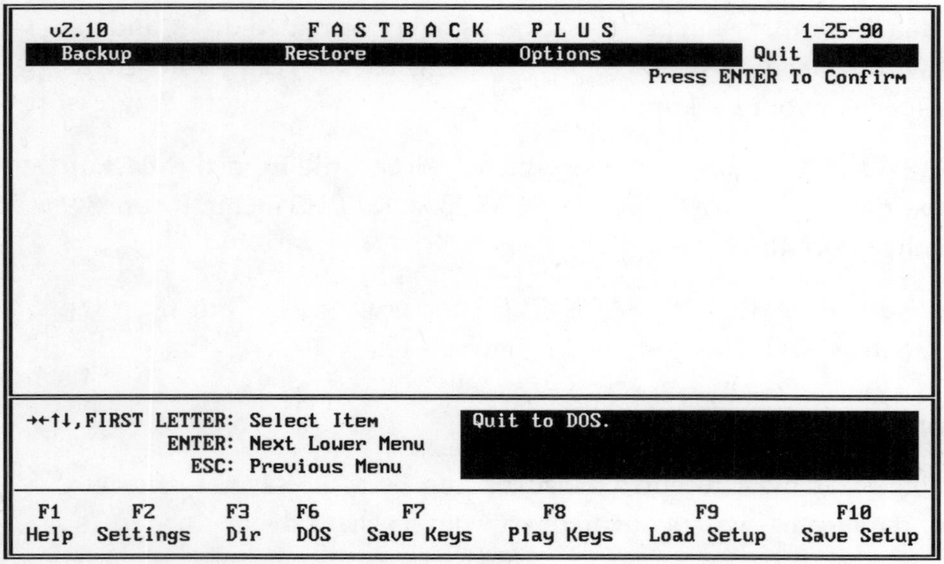

```
 v2.10               F A S T B A C K   P L U S          1-25-90
  Backup           Restore          Options          Quit
                                              Press ENTER To Confirm










 →←↑↓,FIRST LETTER: Select Item      Quit to DOS.
              ENTER: Next Lower Menu
                ESC: Previous Menu

  F1      F2       F3    F6     F7         F8         F9          F10
 Help   Settings  Dir   DOS   Save Keys  Play Keys  Load Setup  Save Setup
```

Normally, you would only want to *immediately* restore your complete full backups in order to return your hard disk to an unfragmented state. In other words, you would use a full restore to *rearrange* the files on your hard disk, thereby restoring the disk to its most efficient state, rather than to actually *replace* the information on the disk.

To do this, you would first use the Compare Files feature on the Start Restore menu to make sure the files you are restoring are the same as the files on your hard disk. You would then reformat your hard disk before beginning the restore procedure.

For now, we will just make a full restore without reformatting your hard disk.

**Step 1**   If you have not already started up FASTBACK PLUS, do so now by typing FB and pressing ENTER at your DOS command prompt:

```
C:>FB
```

**Step 2**   Select the Restore menu from the Main FASTBACK PLUS menu as shown in Figure 8-11.

**Step 3**   Select **Start Restore** from the Restore menu. Figure 8-12 shows the Start Restore menu.

The Main FASTBACK PLUS menu is replaced by the Restore Progress menu, which offers a number of selections on a menu bar at the top of the screen.

Get History and Compare Files are features that you may find useful for later restore procedures. As we've already mentioned, you can use Compare Files to compare the files on your backup floppies to the files on your hard disk, before performing a restore. Get History takes the history file from your backup set and restores it to the support directory on your hard disk in order to do a "smart restore"—in which FASTBACK PLUS automatically selects the most recent version of a backed up file to restore. For more information on either of these features, see the Restore

*Figure 8-11: The Restore Menu*

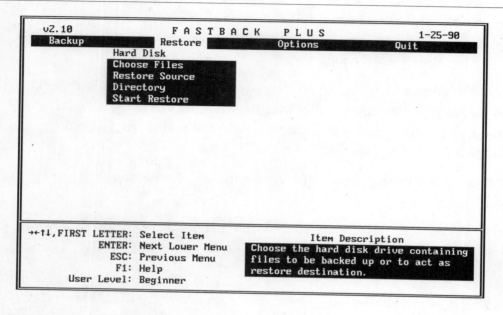

*Figure 8-12: Time and Volumes for a Restore are Estimated*

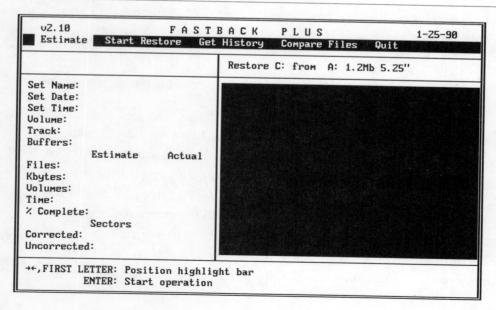

Menu in Chapter 6. We will not be using these features for this sample restore.

**Step 4**   Select **Estimate** from the Restore Progress menu. Figure 8-13 shows what your screen should look like.

*Figure 8-13: Restore Estimate Completed*

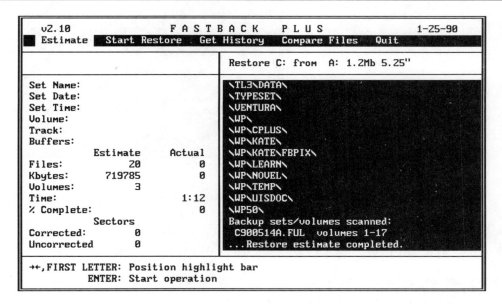

```
  v2.10              F A S T B A C K    P L U S        1-25-90
 ▌ Estimate   Start Restore    Get History    Compare Files    Quit

                                 Restore C: from   A: 1.2Mb 5.25"

 Set Name:                       \TL3\DATA\
 Set Date:                       \TYPESET\
 Set Time:                       \VENTURA\
 Volume:                         \WP\
 Track:                          \WP\CPLUS\
 Buffers:                        \WP\KATE\
             Estimate   Actual   \WP\KATE\FBPIX\
 Files:            20        0   \WP\LEARN\
 Kbytes:       719785        0   \WP\NOVEL\
 Volumes:           3            \WP\TEMP\
 Time:                    1:12   \WP\UISDOC\
 % Complete:                 0   \WP50\
             Sectors             Backup sets/volumes scanned:
 Corrected:         0            C900514A.FUL   volumes 1-17
 Uncorrected        0            ...Restore estimate completed.

 →←,FIRST LETTER: Position highlight bar
           ENTER: Start operation
```

Estimate works similarly to the Estimate feature on the Backup Progress menu. Scanning the selected history files in the support directory on your hard disk, FASTBACK PLUS determines the number and size of the files to be restored, and the name of the required backup set. It also estimates the time required to complete the restore.

When FASTBACK PLUS completes its estimate, we can start the restore process.

**Step 5**   Select **Start Restore** from the Restore Progress menu.

*Figure 8-14: Beginning the Restore*

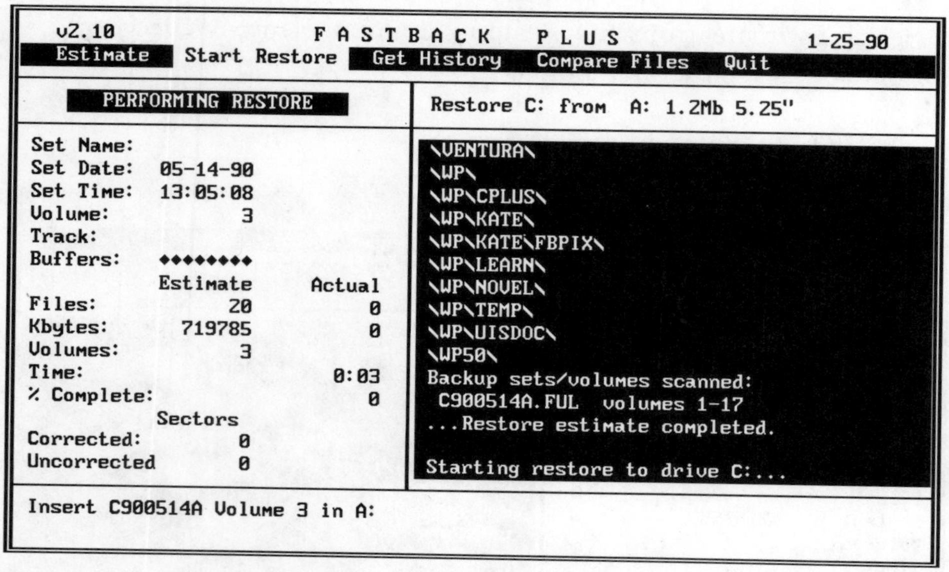

```
 v2.10                F A S T B A C K   P L U S          1-25-90
  Estimate   Start Restore   Get History   Compare Files   Quit

   ┌─── PERFORMING RESTORE ───┐      Restore C: from  A: 1.2Mb 5.25"

  Set Name:                         \VENTURA\
  Set Date:   05-14-90              \WP\
  Set Time:   13:05:08              \WP\CPLUS\
  Volume:            3              \WP\KATE\
  Track:                            \WP\KATE\FBPIX\
  Buffers:    ◆◆◆◆◆◆◆◆              \WP\LEARN\
               Estimate   Actual    \WP\NOVEL\
  Files:            20        0     \WP\TEMP\
  Kbytes:       719785        0     \WP\UISDOC\
  Volumes:           3              \WP50\
  Time:                    0:03     Backup sets/volumes scanned:
  % Complete:               0         C900514A.FUL  volumes 1-17
               Sectors             ...Restore estimate completed.
  Corrected:         0
  Uncorrected        0              Starting restore to drive C:...

  Insert C900514A Volume 3 in A:
```

FASTBACK PLUS prompts you to insert the first volume of the selected backup set in the appropriate floppy disk drive as shown in Figure 8-14.

Before inserting a disk, be sure to check that its backup set name and volume number are the correct ones.

**Step 6**   Insert the first volume of your backup set in the specified drive, and then switch volumes as prompted until the restore is completed.

As with the backup procedure, FASTBACK PLUS will continue prompting you to insert the next volume of the backup set until the restore is complete. Each prompt will be sounded by a beep.

Again, FASTBACK PLUS reports its progress in the Actual column on the left side of the screen. In addition to the information on the files and volumes completed, FASTBACK PLUS tells you whether it has had to correct any disk sectors.

FASTBACK PLUS will tell you when all the backup files from this set have been successfully restored.

**Step 7** Select Quit from the Restore Progress menu to return to the Main FASTBACK PLUS menu. If you want to leave FASTBACK PLUS for now, select Quit from the Main menu as well.

# CHAPTER 9

# *Automatic Partial Backups*

If you have already made your first full backup (perhaps by using the tutorial in Chapter 8), and you are ready to make a partial backup of files that have changed since then, you can use the tutorial in this chapter as a guide.

Making automatic partial backups (that is, partial backups where FAST-BACK PLUS selects the files by using automatic criteria) is almost as easy as making a full backup. You can still use most of FASTBACK PLUS's default settings. The only difference is that you have to change the backup type from **Full** to either **Incremental** or **Differential**.

**Step 1**    If you have not already started up FASTBACK PLUS, do so now by typing FB and pressing ENTER at your DOS command prompt:

C:>FB

**Step 2**    Select **Backup Type** from the Backup menu as shown in Figure 9-1.

The basic options for backup type, **Full**, **Incremental**, and **Differential** are displayed in a pop-up menu, as shown in Figure 9-2.

*Figure 9-1: For a Partial Backup, Select Backup Type*

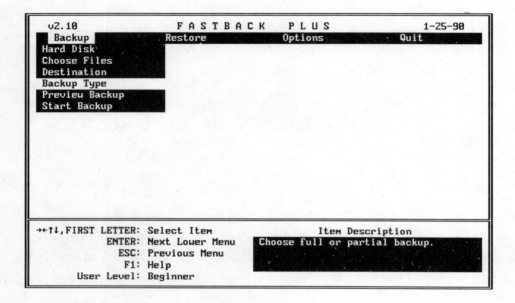

**Step 3**    Select the partial backup type you want: Incremental or Differential.

Remember, an incremental backup backs up only those files that have changed since the *last incremental* backup and a differential backup backs up all files that have changed since the *last full* backup.

Of course, since this is your first partial backup of any kind, either selection is going to back up the files you have changed since you made a full backup in Chapter 8. But in general, you should choose the partial backup type that best suits your needs and workstyle. (For guidelines on choosing a backup strategy, see Chapter 3.)

For this tutorial, choose Incremental.

*Figure 9-2: The Backup Type List*

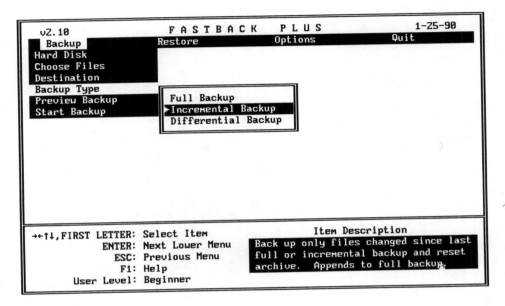

Note: you can also choose **Full Copy** and **Separate Incremental** from this menu by first selecting **Full** or **Incremental**, respectively. See Chapter 5, The Backup Menu, for more details.

**Step 4**  Select **Start Backup** from the Backup menu.

The Backup Progress menu replaces the Main FASTBACK PLUS menu on your screen. Figure 9-3 shows the Backup Progress menu.

Again, you can start your backup immediately, or use the Estimate feature to first get an estimate of the time and number of disks that will be required to complete your partial backup.

Since we used the Estimate feature in our Full Backup tutorial, we will skip it this time. But it is a good idea to use it regularly with each backup both to avoid being caught short of time or disks and to get the backup progress reporting, which FASTBACK PLUS doesn't do unless you have done the estimate.

*Figure 9-3: You Can Use Estimate for Partial Backups Too*

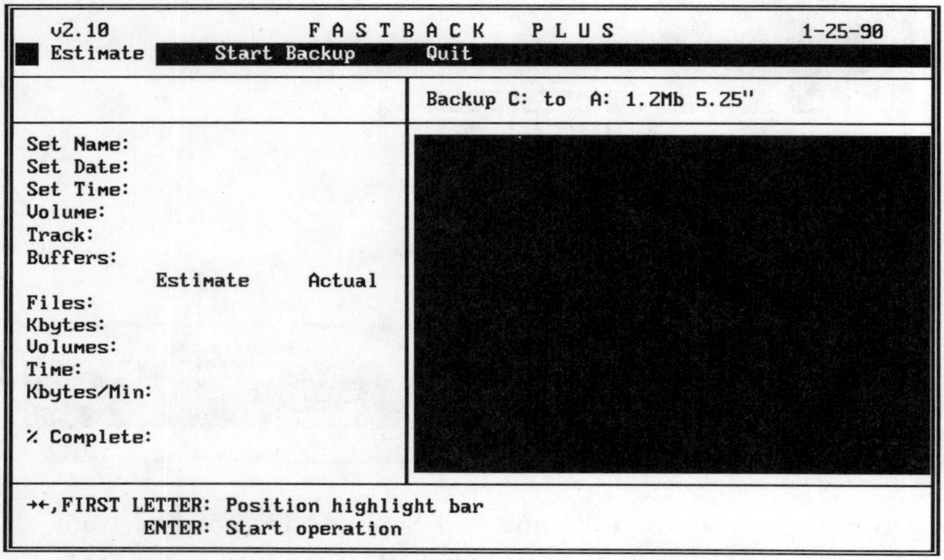

```
 v2.10              F A S T B A C K    P L U S          1-25-90
 Estimate      Start Backup        Quit

                              Backup C: to  A: 1.2Mb 5.25"

 Set Name:
 Set Date:
 Set Time:
 Volume:
 Track:
 Buffers:
              Estimate      Actual
 Files:
 Kbytes:
 Volumes:
 Time:
 Kbytes/Min:

 % Complete:

 →←,FIRST LETTER: Position highlight bar
          ENTER: Start operation
```

**Step 5**   As an added precaution, check your floppy disk drives now to make sure you have not left a disk in them. Any disk in the backup drive when you begin the backup will be overwritten!

**Step 6**   Select **Start Backup** from the Backup Progress menu.

Because we elected not to use the Estimate feature this time, you will not see the backup progress information that you saw when you made your full backup in Chapter 8.

**Step 7**   Follow FASTBACK PLUS's prompts for inserting and removing floppy disks as each one gets filled up with your backed up files.

Remember, FASTBACK PLUS automatically formats any floppy disk that needs formatting, so you don't have to.

At the sound of the beep, you will be prompted to insert Volume 2, Volume 3, and so on, each time FASTBACK PLUS is ready for you to insert a new floppy disk.

**Step 8** As you did with the Full backup in Chapter 8, label each backup disk as you remove it from the drive. Every backup disk you make should have the correct Set Name and Volume number on it.

**Step 9** When your partial backup is complete, select **Quit** from the Backup Progress menu to return to the Main FASTBACK PLUS menu. Figure 9-4 shows what your screen will look like when the backup is complete.

If you want to leave FASTBACK PLUS for now, select **Quit** from the Main menu as well—see Figure 9-5.

*Figure 9-4: The Partial Backup is Completed*

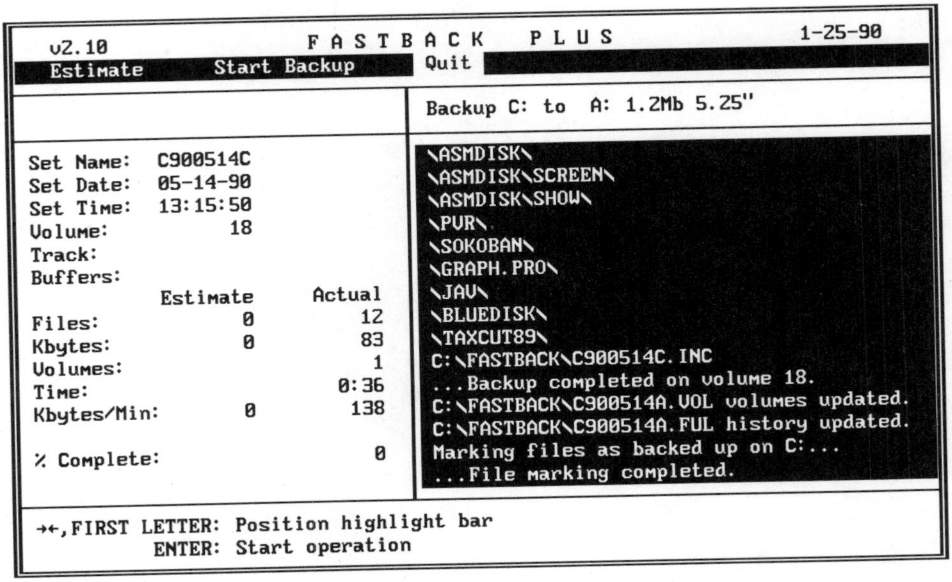

```
   v2.10                 F A S T B A C K    P L U S        1-25-90
   Estimate        Start Backup      Quit

                               Backup C: to  A: 1.2Mb 5.25"

   Set Name:  C900514C              \ASMDISK\
   Set Date:  05-14-90              \ASMDISK\SCREEN\
   Set Time:  13:15:50              \ASMDISK\SHOW\
   Volume:         18               \PUR\
   Track:                           \SOKOBAN\
   Buffers:                         \GRAPH.PRO\
              Estimate    Actual    \JAV\
   Files:          0         12     \BLUEDISK\
   Kbytes:         0         83     \TAXCUT89\
   Volumes:                   1     C:\FASTBACK\C900514C.INC
   Time:                   0:36      ...Backup completed on volume 18.
   Kbytes/Min:     0        138     C:\FASTBACK\C900514A.VOL volumes updated.
                                    C:\FASTBACK\C900514A.FUL history updated.
   % Complete:                0     Marking files as backed up on C:...
                                     ...File marking completed.

   →←,FIRST LETTER: Position highlight bar
                ENTER: Start operation
```

*Figure 9-5: Select Quit to Leave FASTBACK PLUS*

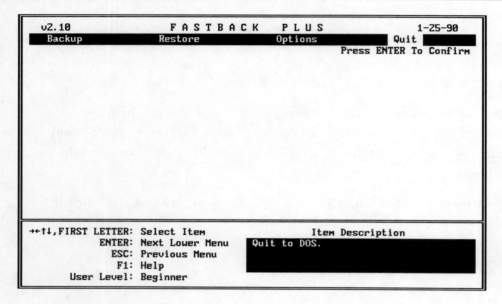

# CHAPTER 10

# *Individual Files and Directories*

This chapter will guide you through the process of selecting exactly those files you want to include in a backup or restore procedure and then saving the list of files in a special kind of FASTBACK PLUS file called a *setup file.* Since the steps required for actually doing a backup and a restore are covered in Chapters 8 and 9, we will concentrate here only on the steps required for file selection. Note that the procedures outlined in this chapter work the same for both backup and restore file selection.

For more details on the file selection methods and procedures used in this chapter, see Chapter 2.

Here is a brief outline of the procedures we will follow in this tutorial:

1. First, we will compile a list of files to *include,* using the Choose Files feature on the Beginner Backup menu. We will add directories and files to this include list by typing them directly into the Choose Files to Include window.
2. Next, we will change the User Level to Advanced and narrow down our include list by specifying some files to *exclude* from that list, using Exclude Files from the Backup menu. This time, we'll

try the Directory Tree feature that is always available when you are doing any kind of file selection in FASTBACK PLUS.

3. To narrow our list a little further, we will filter it through a Date Gate created with the Files by Date feature from the Advanced level Backup menu.

4. Finally, we will save our list of files in a FASTBACK PLUS setup file so that they can be re-used in future backups.

**Step 1**   Select **Choose Files** from the Backup menu.

At the Beginner level, the Backup and Restore menus offer only one filter for selecting files: Choose Files. Choose Files allows you to actively identify each directory, partial directory or individual file you want to include in the list of files you will back up or restore. Choose Files is shown in Figure 10-1.

*Figure 10-1: Choose Files on the Beginner Menu*

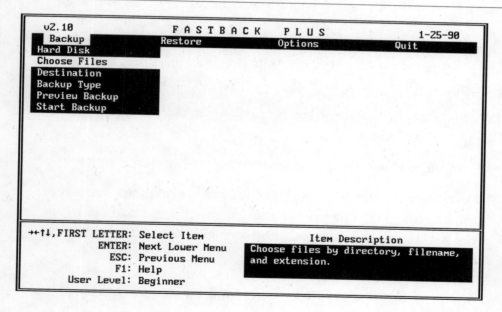

Remember that the Experienced and Advanced menus also offer the Choose Files filter, only under a different name: Include Files. Include Files works exactly the same way as Choose Files; there is no difference except in the name.

When you have selected Choose Files, a window entitled **Choose Files To Include** appears at the bottom of your screen, below the menu, as shown in Figure 10-2.

*Figure 10-2: The Choose Files To Include Window*

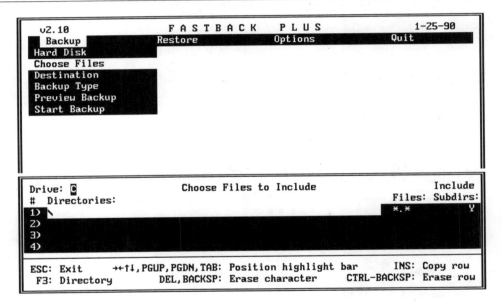

This is where FASTBACK PLUS lists the files you select for your current backup or restore procedure. Notice that the source drive is identified in the top, left-hand corner of the window. In the case of a backup, this is the letter designation of your hard disk; in the case of a restore, it names one of your floppy drives.

Across the next line of the window, you see the following columns:

- **#**   The line number. The window has 20 lines.
- **Directories:**  The directory name for the current line. The default directory is simply a \, which indicates the *Root* directory of your hard disk.
- **Files:**  The name of a file or group of files (via wildcard designations). FASTBACK PLUS supplies a wildcard string as a default for Files. This means "all files in the designated directory."
- **Include Subdirs:**  Whether to include all subdirectories of this directory. The default is Y (Yes). If you want to ignore subdirectories of a particular directory, change the Y to N.

The default selection that FASTBACK PLUS supplies, \ *.* Y, is meant to include all directories and files on the designated hard disk—in other words, FASTBACK PLUS will make a full backup by default.

**Step 2**   To clear the first line in the Choose Files window, press CTRL-BACKSPACE. Figure 10-3 shows line 1 cleared.

*Figure 10-3: Line 1 is Cleared When You Press CTRL-BACKSPACE*

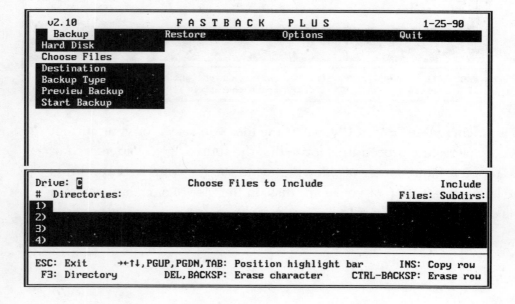

**Step 3**  Now type \ and the name of the first directory from which you want to include files. Figure 10-4 shows an example of what your screen may look like.

*Figure 10-4: First, Enter a Directory Name*

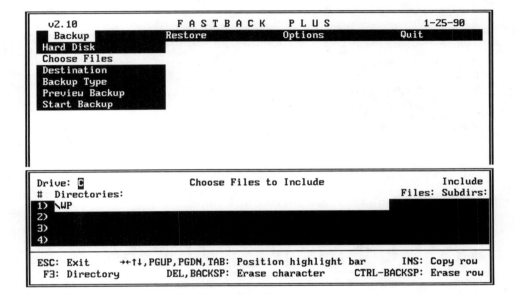

```
 v2.10                 F A S T B A C K   P L U S        1-25-90
   Backup            Restore           Options          Quit
 Hard Disk
 Choose Files
 Destination
 Backup Type
 Preview Backup
 Start Backup




 Drive: C            Choose Files to Include            Include
 #  Directories:                             Files: Subdirs:
 1) \WP
 2)
 3)
 4)
 ESC: Exit      →←↑↓,PGUP,PGDN,TAB: Position highlight bar    INS: Copy row
   F3: Directory        DEL,BACKSP: Erase character  CTRL-BACKSP: Erase row
```

**Step 4**  To move over to the Files: column, press TAB, as shown in Figure 10-5.

**Step 5**  Type a file designation. This can be:

- A single filename (for example, FBCHAP1.WP)
- A wildcard filename with a specific file extension (for example, *.WP specifies all files with the .WP extension)
- A specific filename with a wildcard file extension (for example, FBCHAP1.* specifies all files with the name FBCHAP1, but different file extensions)
- A wildcard combination that names several files with the same extension (for example, FBCHAP*.WP specifies all files whose

names *begin* with the string FBCHAP and who have an extension of .WP)

■ A full wildcard string, such as the default string *.*, which specifies all files in the designated directory

*Figure 10-5: Next, Tab Over to Files*

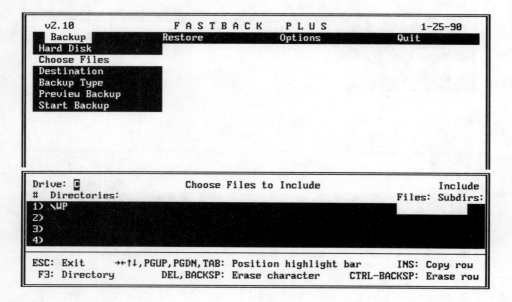

For our current procedure, we will include all files in the \WP directory by using the full wildcard string, as shown in Figure 10-6.

**Step 6**  Leaving the Include Subdirs: column as is for this pathname, press ENTER to confirm the pathname and begin again at Line 2. Figure 10-7 shows what your screen would look like.

**Step 7**  Repeat steps 3 through 6, until you have included all the directories and files you want to back up or restore.

Remember the following as you enter new pathnames:

*Figure 10-6: Whole Directory Specified by Wildcard String*

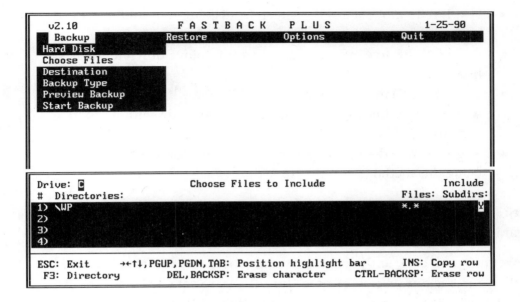

*Figure 10-7: Now press ENTER to Move the Next Line*

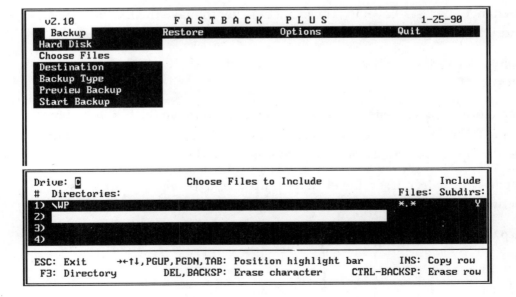

- Use the UP and DOWN arrow keys to scroll forward or backward through your list of files.
- Use TAB to move *across* the screen from column to column as you enter pathnames.
- Press ENTER to confirm a pathname and move down to the next line.
- The Choose Files window contains 20 lines. If you need to use more than 20 lines, you will have to begin again with a separate backup set.
- You can include anything from entire directories to single files using this method.

**Step 8**   To save your list of files and leave the Choose Files To Include window, press ESC.

This takes you back to the Backup menu, where you can either proceed with your backup or restore procedure if you're satisfied with the list you've compiled, or refine your list by specifying files to exclude.

We will go on now to exclude some files from our list. But first we have to change the User Level to Advanced in order to make the Exclude Files and Files by Date features available on the menus.

**Step 9**   Move the highlight bar to **User Level** on the Options menu and press ENTER.

Remember, you can either use the Arrow keys to move the highlight bar or press the first letter of the selection you want—in this case, press **O** to get the Options menu, then press **U** to select User Level.

When you select User Level, a pop-up menu of choices appears as shown in Figure 10-8.

**Step 10**   Select **Advanced** from the pop-up menu.

*Figure 10-8: Select the User Level Menu to Change User Level*

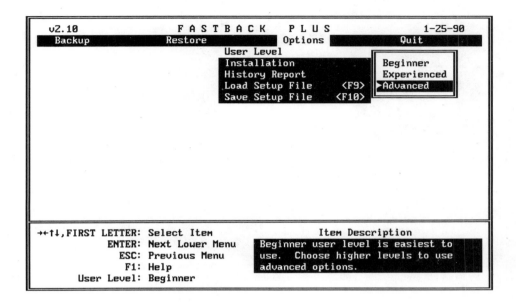

```
  v2.10                   F A S T B A C K   P L U S              1-25-90
     Backup              Restore            Options              Quit
                                   User Level
                              Installation                  Beginner
                              History Report                Experienced
                             .Load Setup File      <F9>    ►Advanced
                              Save Setup File      <F10>




  ↦←↑↓,FIRST LETTER: Select Item                     Item Description
            ENTER: Next Lower Menu        Beginner user level is easiest to
              ESC: Previous Menu          use.  Choose higher levels to use
               F1: Help                   advanced options.
       User Level: Beginner
```

Now the full list of FASTBACK PLUS features is available to you. Figure 10-9 shows the Advanced Backup menu.

**Step 11**    Move back to the Backup menu and select **Exclude Files**. The screen shown in Figure 10-10 will appear.

A window entitled **Choose Files to Exclude** appears at the bottom of the screen.

Exclude Files uses the same methods of file selection available to Choose Files and Include Files. The difference is that Exclude Files creates a list of files to be *excluded* from the list you have already made of files to be *included*.

The current include files list may be one automatically created by FAST-BACK PLUS for a full or automatic partial backup or restore, or it may

*Figure 10-9: The Advanced Backup Menu*

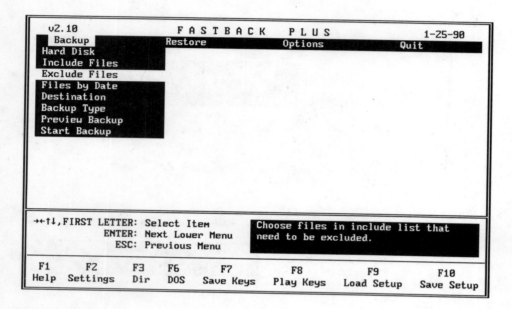

*Figure 10-10: The Choose Files To Exclude Window*

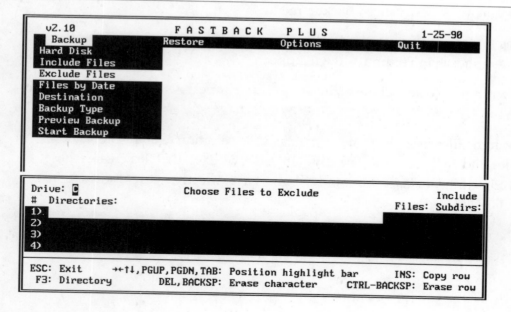

be one you created yourself, using the steps outlined above. In either case, Exclude Files always *modifies* the Include Files list.

For the purpose of this tutorial, we will use the Directory Tree method to select files for exclusion.

Note that you do not need to explicitly add files to your Exclude list that you have not Included with Include Files; FASTBACK PLUS automatically excludes anything not explicitly included.

**Step 12**   To get a Directory Tree of your files, press F3. Your screen should look similar to the one shown in Figure 10-11.

*Figure 10-11: A Sample Directory Tree of Drive C*

```
┌══════ \WP\KATE ═══════════════════════════════════════════════════
│   ├─TASM                  ►ALTE     .WPM ►AVANTDOC.TXT ►BECKY    .LET
│   │  └─TAP                ►BENCH1   .STA ►EDITOR   .ENV ►EDITOR   .JOB
│   ├─TAXCUT89              ►EISDOC   .TXT ►EISDOC1  .TXT ►EISINTR  .TXT
│   ├─TD                    ►EISMEMO  .TXT ►EISUP    .CAP ►EISUP    .CHP
│   ├─TL3                   ►EISUP    .CIF ►EISUP    .TXT ►EISUP    .UGR
│   │  └─DATA               ►FBAPXA   .WP  ►FBCHAP1  .WP  ►FBCHAP10.WP
│   ├─TYPESET               ►FBCHAP11.WP  ►FBCHAP2  .WP  ►FBCHAP3  .WP
│   ├─VENTURA               ►FBCHAP4  .WP  ►FBCHAP5  .WP  ►FBCHAP6  .WP
│   ►WP                     ►FBCHAP7  .WP  ►FBCHAP8  .WP  ►FBCHAP9  .WP
│      ├─►CPLUS             ►FBFILES  .TXT ►FBPARIII.WP  ►FBPARTI  .WP
│      ├─►KATE              ►FBPARTII.WP  ►FBPLUS   .OUT ►GIGI     .LET
│      │  └─►FBPIX          ►GIGI     .RES ►GLADYS   .LET ►GPDONOR3.LET
│      ├─►LEARN             ►GPDONOR4.LET ►GPDONOR5.LET ►GPDONOR6.LET
├─────────────────────────────────────────────────────────────────────
│ Drive: C          Choose Files to Exclude              Include
│ #  Directories:                              Files: Subdirs:
│ 1)
│ 2)
│ 3)
│ 4)
├─────────────────────────────────────────────────────────────────────
│ ESC: Exit          →←↑↓,PGUP,PGDN,HOME,END: Move highlight bar in window
│ INS: Copy filespec  TAB: Move highlight bar to file or directory window
```

A directory tree is a graphical display of a directory and its subdirectories. It appears at the top of your screen when you press F3, temporarily replacing the FASTBACK PLUS menu.

As the new key mapping at the bottom of your screen indicates, you can use the arrow keys to scroll both vertically and horizontally through the directory tree.

**Step 13** To exclude a whole directory from your list of files, highlight that directory and press INS.

FASTBACK PLUS automatically copies the directory name with a wildcard file designation into the next available line of the Choose Files To Exclude window.

We only want to exclude certain files from this directory, so we will edit the wildcard string in the Files: column. Figure 10-12 shows a highlighted directory in the directory tree and directory name with a wildcard string in the Choose Files to Exclude window.

*Figure 10-12: Highlight a Directory and Press INS to Add It*

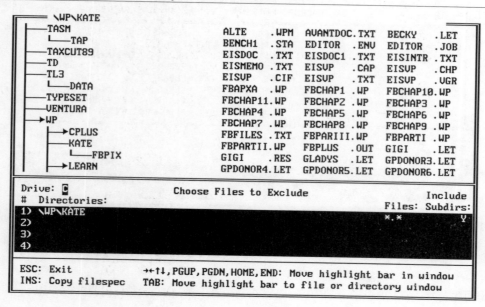

**Step 14** Press ESC to exit the Directory Tree and activate the Choose Files To Exclude window, as shown in Figure 10-13.

*Figure 10-13: Press ESC to Move Cursor Back to Exclude Files*

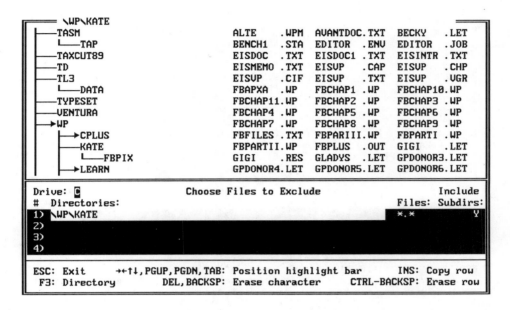

```
┌────────────────────────────────────────────────────────────────────────┐
│ ┌───── \WP\KATE                                                          │
│ ├──TASM              ALTE      .WPM  AVANTDOC.TXT  BECKY    .LET          │
│ │   └──TAP           BENCH1    .STA  EDITOR   .ENV  EDITOR   .JOB         │
│ ├──TAXCUT89          EISDOC    .TXT  EISDOC1  .TXT  EISINTR  .TXT         │
│ ├──TD                EISMEMO   .TXT  EISUP    .CAP  EISUP    .CHP         │
│ ├──TL3               EISUP     .CIF  EISUP    .TXT  EISUP    .VGR         │
│ │   └──DATA          FBAPXA    .WP   FBCHAP1  .WP   FBCHAP10.WP           │
│ ├──TYPESET           FBCHAP11.WP    FBCHAP2  .WP   FBCHAP3 .WP            │
│ ├──VENTURA           FBCHAP4   .WP   FBCHAP5  .WP   FBCHAP6 .WP           │
│ └►WP                 FBCHAP7   .WP   FBCHAP8  .WP   FBCHAP9 .WP           │
│     ├►CPLUS          FBFILES   .TXT  FBPARIII.WP   FBPARTI .WP            │
│     ├──KATE          FBPARTII.WP    FBPLUS   .OUT  GIGI    .LET           │
│     │   └──FBPIX     GIGI      .RES  GLADYS   .LET  GPDONOR3.LET          │
│     ├►LEARN          GPDONOR4.LET   GPDONOR5.LET   GPDONOR6.LET           │
├────────────────────────────────────────────────────────────────────────┤
│ Drive: C              Choose Files to Exclude              Include        │
│ #   Directories:                                      Files: Subdirs:    │
│ 1) \WP\KATE                                            *.*           Y    │
│ 2)                                                                        │
│ 3)                                                                        │
│ 4)                                                                        │
├────────────────────────────────────────────────────────────────────────┤
│ ESC:  Exit      ←↑↓,PGUP,PGDN,TAB: Position highlight bar    INS: Copy row│
│  F3:  Directory        DEL,BACKSP: Erase character   CTRL-BACKSP: Erase row│
└────────────────────────────────────────────────────────────────────────┘
```

**Step 15**   Press TAB to move to the Files: column, as shown in Figure 10-14.

**Step 16**   Edit the wildcard string to specify only the files from this directory that you actually want to exclude from your list. Figure 10-15 shows the edited wildcard string.

We will exclude all the files in the \WP directory with a file extension of .LET.

**Step 17**   Repeat steps 12 and 13 to exclude more directories and files if you wish, using steps 14 through 16 to edit pathnames as necessary.

When a directory is highlighted, its files are listed to the right of the tree. To add individual files to your list, first press TAB to switch the highlight bar to the files list. Then you can scroll through the files list and select individual files by highlighting them and pressing INS. Again, FASTBACK

*Figure 10-14: Press TAB to Move the Cursor Over to Files*

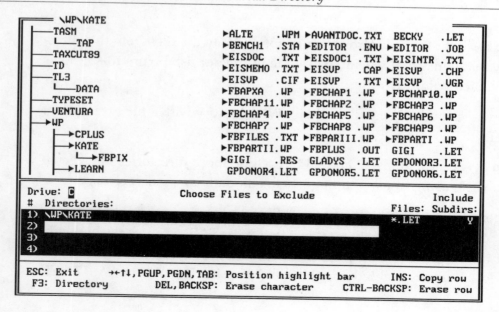

*Figure 10-15: Edit the Wildcard to Exclude Partial Directory*

PLUS copies the pathname of the file into the Choose Files To Exclude window. You can switch back to the directory tree anytime by pressing TAB again. Figure 10-16 shows a screen during individual file selection.

*Figure 10-16: Selecting Individual File from Directory Tree*

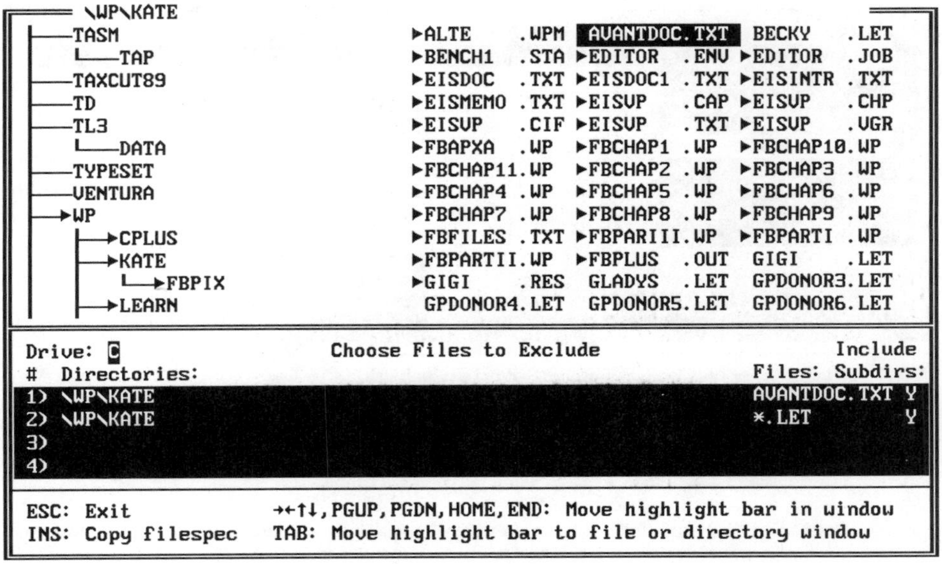

```
═══  \WP\KATE
  ├──TASM           ►ALTE    .WPM  AVANTDOC.TXT  BECKY    .LET
  │   └──TAP        ►BENCH1  .STA ►EDITOR  .ENV ►EDITOR   .JOB
  ├──TAXCUT89       ►EISDOC  .TXT ►EISDOC1 .TXT ►EISINTR .TXT
  ├──TD             ►EISMEMO .TXT ►EISUP   .CAP ►EISUP   .CHP
  ├──TL3            ►EISUP   .CIF ►EISUP   .TXT ►EISUP   .VGR
  │   └──DATA       ►FBAPXA  .WP  ►FBCHAP1 .WP  ►FBCHAP10.WP
  ├──TYPESET        ►FBCHAP11.WP  ►FBCHAP2 .WP  ►FBCHAP3 .WP
  ├──VENTURA        ►FBCHAP4 .WP  ►FBCHAP5 .WP  ►FBCHAP6 .WP
  ├─►WP             ►FBCHAP7 .WP  ►FBCHAP8 .WP  ►FBCHAP9 .WP
  │   ├─►CPLUS      ►FBFILES .TXT ►FBPARIII.WP  ►FBPARTI .WP
  │   ├─►KATE       ►FBPARTII.WP  ►FBPLUS  .OUT  GIGI    .LET
  │   │  └─►FBPIX   ►GIGI    .RES  GLADYS  .LET  GPDONOR3.LET
  │   ├─►LEARN       GPDONOR4.LET GPDONOR5.LET GPDONOR6.LET
  ├────────────────────────────────────────────────────────
  │ Drive: C        Choose Files to Exclude        Include
  │ #  Directories:                            Files: Subdirs:
  │ 1) \WP\KATE                                AVANTDOC.TXT Y
  │ 2) \WP\KATE                                *.LET        Y
  │ 3)
  │ 4)
  ├────────────────────────────────────────────────────────
  │ ESC: Exit       →←↑↓,PGUP,PGDN,HOME,END: Move highlight bar in window
  │ INS: Copy filespec   TAB: Move highlight bar to file or directory window
```

**Step 18**   When you are satisfied with your list of exclusions, press ESC to return to the Backup menu.

The Advanced Backup menu offers one final file selection filter we should try: **Files by Date**. Like Exclude Files, you use Files by Date after you have made your list of files to Include (and Exclude) to further narrow the set of files you want to back up or restore. Figure 10-17 shows the Files by Date Filter as it appears on the Advanced menu.

**Step 19**   Select **Files by Date** from the Backup menu.

A series of prompts guides you through the creation of a *Date Gate*. The Date Gate excludes files created before and after certain dates that FAST-BACK PLUS prompts you to specify. Thus, you can narrow down the files on your Include list to only those files that were created within the specified period, or Date Gate. FASTBACK PLUS prompts you through the creation of a Date Gate, as shown in Figure 10-18.

*Figure 10-17: Files by Date on the Advanced Menu*

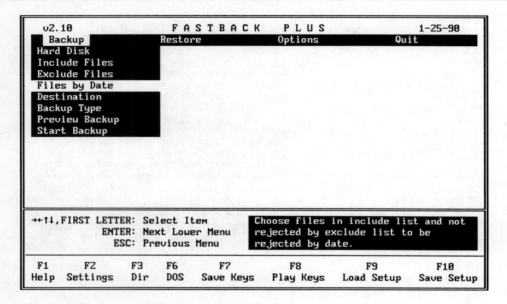

**Step 20**   Enter before and after dates as FASTBACK PLUS prompts you for them, using the format MM-DD-YY, as shown in Figure 10-19.

FASTBACK PLUS then asks if you want to *Use these date gates?*

**Step 21**   Figure 10-20 shows a completed Date Gate. Answer Y.

Now we have a completely customized list of files to include in a backup or restore procedure. Let's save this list of files in a *setup file* (you'll learn more about setup files in the next few chapters) so we'll have it on file for future backups.

**Step 22**   Press F10 to save these settings in a setup file.

*Figure 10-18: Creating a Date Gate*

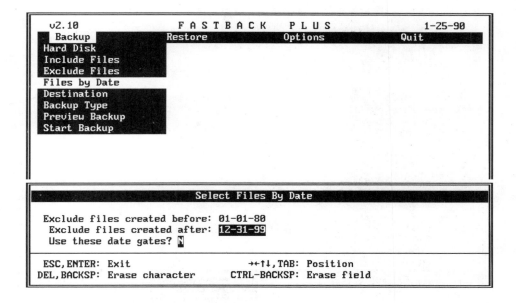

*Figure 10-19: Enter New Dates*

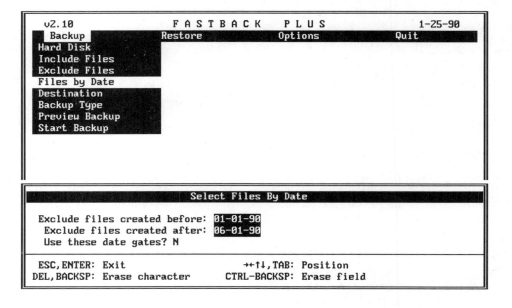

*Figure 10-20: The Completed Date Gate*

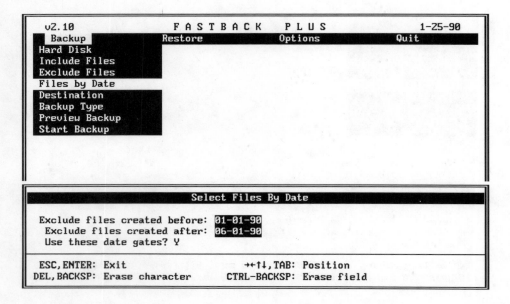

Note: at the Advanced level, **Save Setup File** is available only by pressing F10; it does not appear on the Options menu.

FASTBACK PLUS prompts you for a filename to save the current settings under, as shown in Figure 10-21.

**Step 23**   Type a valid DOS pathname specifying the directory, subdirectory (if applicable), and filename you want to use for this setup file. Figure 10-22 shows an example.

The filename should have an extension of .FB. (Remember—you can press CTRL-BACKSPACE to erase the default.)

Since we want to save *only* our file selections for now, we can use the Save Filespecs Only? option.

**Step 24**   Press TAB to move to the **Save filespecs only?** field, and change the N to a Y. Figure 10-23 shows what your screen will look like.

*Figure 10-21: CTRL-BACKSPACE Erases Default Setup Filename*

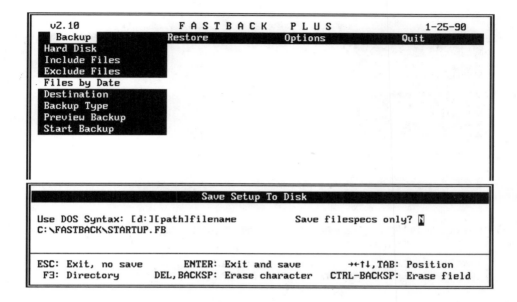

*Figure 10-22: Enter a New Setup Filename*

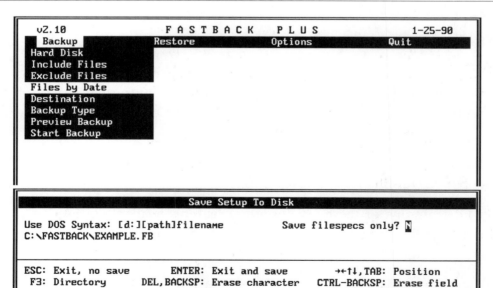

*Figure 10-23: Press TAB to Move to Save Filespecs Only*

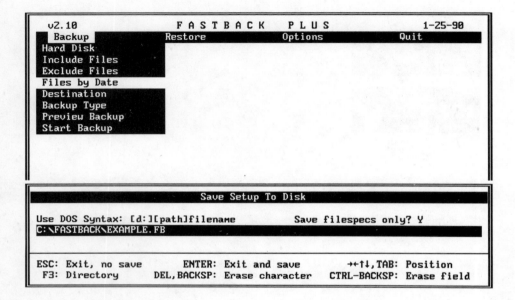

**Step 25**   Press ENTER to save these settings to the file named EXAM-PLE.FB.

One final step:

**Step 26**   Either select **Quit** from the Main FASTBACK PLUS menu, or go on to Chapter 11 for a short tutorial on a different way to save FAST-BACK PLUS settings.

Note: if you don't feel comfortable staying at the Advanced Level, select **User Level** from the Options menu and change the setting back to **Beginner** before **Quit**ting FASTBACK PLUS.

Setup Files are one of the most important features available in FAST-BACK PLUS. By using Setup Files, you don't have to go through the time-consuming process of selecting each setting every time you use FASTBACK PLUS.

You may want to create many different Setup Files for the different types of backups and restores you perform on a regular basis. This may mean you have different Setup Files for different days of the week or for incremental backups.

# CHAPTER 11

# *Saving and Playing Back a Keystroke Sequence*

When you run FASTBACK PLUS, all the menu selections are set to their default settings automatically, using a *setup file* called STARTUP.FB. STARTUP.FB was created when you installed FASTBACK PLUS, but FASTBACK PLUS allows you to create your own setup files as often you wish—each with a different set of FASTBACK PLUS menu settings.

There are two ways to save FASTBACK PLUS settings for later use—in a *setup file* or in a *keystroke macro*. The difference between them is not in the result, but in when and how they are created:

To create a setup file, you go through the procedure you want, making menu selections, and changing settings as you go along. Then, as we did in the tutorial on selecting files (Chapter 10), you can use the **Save Setup** File feature on the Options menu to save the current settings in a file before you leave FASTBACK PLUS. Later, you can use **Load Setup File** to retrieve the file and change all your menu settings to match those in the file.

To create a keystroke macro, you "turn on" a keystroke recording feature by selecting **Keystrokes to File** from the Options menu. Then, as you navigate through your FASTBACK PLUS procedure, every keystroke is dynamically recorded in a file. Later, you can use **Playback Keystrokes** to literally play back every keystroke—you'll actually see menus and screens changing as the keystrokes you recorded are played back.

The net result is the same whether you use Save Setup File or Keystrokes to File: the selections you choose for one procedure can be saved and re-used over and over again.

We used the Save Setup File feature in Chapter 10 when we finished selecting files. In this chapter, we will go through a short keystroke macro just to give you an idea of how it works.

**Step 1**   If you are still at the Beginner user level, select **User Level** from the Options menu and change the level to **Experienced**, as shown in Figure 11-1.

You don't have menu access to the keystroke macro feature at the Beginner level, although it is available to beginners on the F7 key.

**Step 2**   Select Keystrokes to File from the Options menu (or press F7). Figure 11-2 shows Keystrokes to File on the Options menu.

FASTBACK PLUS prompts you for a filename (see Figure 11-3) to save your keystrokes under. As a default, FASTBACK PLUS offers the filename KEYS.FB.

**Step 3**   Type a valid DOS pathname specifying the directory, subdirectory (if applicable), and filename you want to use for this keystroke file, and press ENTER. Figure 11-4 illustrates this procedure.

Remember—you can press CTRL-BACKSPACE to erase the default.

Note: like setup files, keystroke macro files must have a file extension of .FB.

*Figure 11-1: Change the User Level to Experienced*

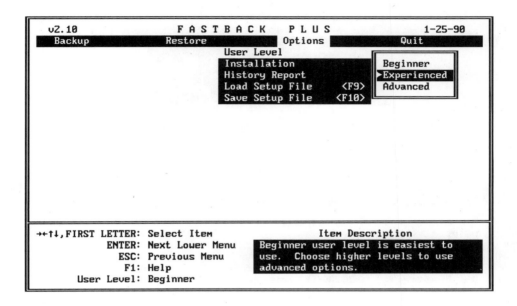

*Figure 11-2: Select Keystrokes to File from Options Menu*

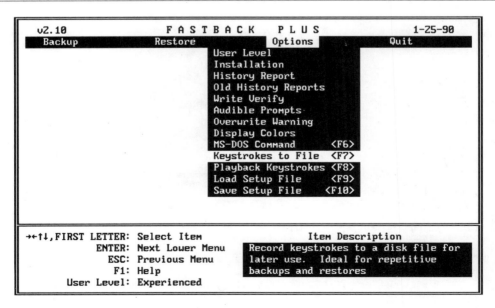

*Figure 11-3: FASTBACK PLUS Prompts for a Filename*

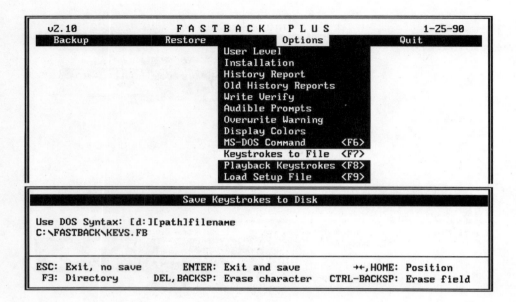

*Figure 11-4: Erase Default, Then Enter Your Own Pathname*

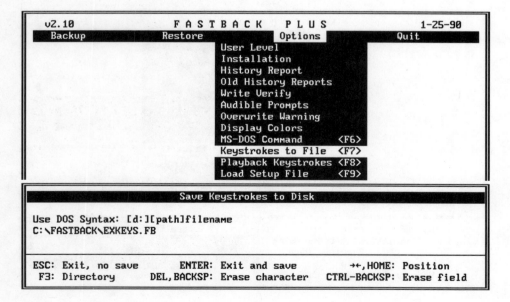

As soon as you press ENTER, the cursor returns to its home position—
the first selection on the FASTBACK PLUS menu.

We'll just change a couple of settings on the Options menu to demonstrate how the keystroke macro works.

**Step 4**   Make the following selections from the FASTBACK PLUS menus:

1. Select Audible Prompts and change the setting to Chime. Figure
   11-5 illustrates this procedure.
2. Select Display Colors and then select Main Menus. When the ele-

*Figure 11-5: Change the Prompt Sound to Chime*

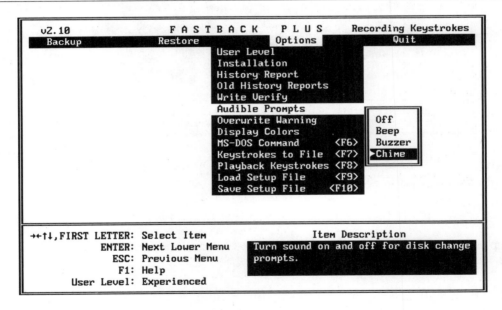

ments of the Main Menus display appear, change the color of each
by highlighting it and then pressing SHIFT-DOWN or SHIFT-UP
to scroll through the available colors until you find one you like.
When you release the scroll key you're using, the current color
will take effect for that element of the menus. Change as many ele-

ments as you like and then press ESC twice to return to the Options menu. This procedure is shown in Figure 11-6.

*Figure 11-6: Change the Display Colors*

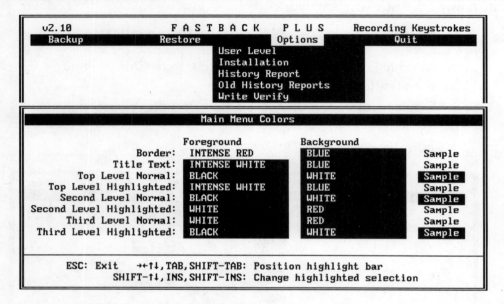

As you make these small changes from the Options menu, every keystroke is recorded in your keystroke macro file.

Now we are ready to save all your keystrokes in the file.

**Step 5**   Select Keystrokes to File from the Options menu again (or press F7).

FASTBACK PLUS displays a message informing you that it has stopped recording your keystrokes to the file, as shown in Figure 11-7.

**Step 6**   Press any key—say, the SPACE bar for instance—to erase this message and go on.

Now let's see what happens when we play back the keystroke macro we just created:

*Figure 11-7: FASTBACK PLUS Responds With a Message*

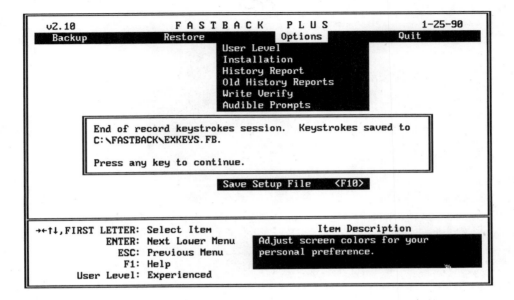

**Step 7** Select **Playback Keystrokes** from the Options menu (or press F8).

FASTBACK PLUS prompts you for the name of the keystroke file to play back, offering the file we just saved as the default. The screen shown in Figure 11-8 appears.

**Step 8** Press ENTER to accept the default keystroke macro file, which should be the one you just saved.

Remember—you can always press CTRL-BACKSPACE to erase the default if you want to play back another file.

FASTBACK PLUS immediately begins to play back the keystrokes in the file, changing the Audible Prompt and Display Colors, just as we did a few minutes ago. This is illustrated in Figure 11-9.

*Figure 11-8: FASTBACK PLUS Prompts for the Filename*

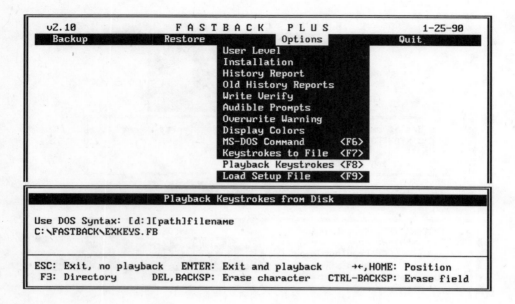

*Figure 11-9: A Point in the Playback*

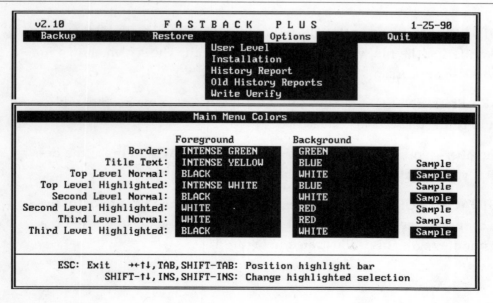

*PART IV*

# *Advanced Features of FASTBACK PLUS*

If you have read the first three parts of this book, you have learned almost everything FASTBACK PLUS can do. In the final two chapters, we will go into a little more detail about some of the more advanced features of FASTBACK PLUS.

Chapters 10 and 11 contained tutorials that guided you through the steps to using *batch files*—setup files and keystroke macros—in FASTBACK PLUS. Chapter 12 examines the *Macro Command Language*, which allows you to create and edit batch files outside of FASTBACK PLUS. This chapter also explains how to execute FASTBACK PLUS batch files from the DOS command line, as well as how to incorporate FASTBACK PLUS commands into DOS batch files.

Chapter 13 takes a more detailed look at some other important features on the Experienced and Advanced level Options menus, including:

- Data Compression
- Error Correction
- Password Protection
- MS-DOS Command

*CHAPTER 12*

# *Using the FASTBACK PLUS Macro Command Language*

The tutorials in Chapters 10 and 11 showed you how to create and execute FASTBACK PLUS setup files and keystroke macros—also known as *batch files*. The underlying facility that makes these powerful FASTBACK PLUS features possible is the *Macro Command Processor*. You don't see it on any of the FASTBACK PLUS menus, but whenever you save or load a setup file, or use Keystrokes to File or Playback Keystrokes, you are seeing the Macro Command Processor at work.

The batch file commands provided to Experienced level users on the Options menu and to Advanced level users as function key assignments, are sufficient to create and execute the most complex batch files in FAST-BACK PLUS. Some users, however, may want the freedom to create batch files outside of FASTBACK PLUS and run them from DOS or incorporate them into DOS batch files. That's why the makers of FAST-BACK PLUS provided the Macro Command Language.

An important part of FASTBACK PLUS's Macro Command Processor, the *Macro Command Language* is a set of code values assigned to the keystrokes that FASTBACK PLUS recognizes as commands. You can use the

Macro Command Language to create batch files in any word processing or text editing program that can produce ASCII text files as output. (Before you use your word processor to create FASTBACK PLUS batch files, check to see if it requires special instructions or conversion routines to output ASCII files.)

This chapter describes the FASTBACK PLUS Macro Command Language and how to use it.

Caution: it is not recommended that you create or edit FASTBACK PLUS batch files outside of FASTBACK PLUS unless you are completely confident of your understanding of the Macro Command Language and your skill as a DOS user.

## Batch Files—A Review

When you record a series of FASTBACK PLUS commands and settings, either in a setup file or a keystroke macro, you are creating a FASTBACK PLUS batch file. You may already be familiar with the batch file concept from using batch files in MS-DOS. Basically, a batch file is just that—a batch of commands, saved in a file, which can be executed just by executing the filename. When you enter the filename, the program reads and executes each command or keystroke in sequence.

Using batch files eliminates the need to remember or write down complex settings or sequences of keystrokes that you use over and over again. Instead, you record them once in a batch file, and then you have them at your fingertips whenever you need them.

FASTBACK PLUS provides two methods of saving settings and keystrokes in batch files:

You can use Save Setup File to save your current FASTBACK PLUS menu settings in a file, and later use Load Setup File to retrieve the file and change all your menu settings to match those in the file.

Or, you can literally record your keystrokes as you make them by selecting Keystrokes to File, and later use Playback Keystrokes to play back every keystroke in the file.

The difference is that when you load a setup file, the FASTBACK PLUS menu settings are all changed "behind the scenes," whereas when you play back a keystroke macro, you actually see every keystroke repeated, with menus and screens flashing by.

## The Macro Command Language

Recall that one method of selecting an item from a FASTBACK PLUS menu is to type the first letter of that item. This moves the highlight bar to the item, and then you can press ENTER to select it.

The FASTBACK PLUS Macro Command Language is based on this "first-letter" method. Each FASTBACK PLUS command or menu selection is represented in the Macro Command Language by its initial letter. Since some menu items share a common first letter (Start Backup and Start Restore, for example), the FASTBACK PLUS Macro Command Processor also needs a to use a simple syntax, in the form of the command context, to interpret certain keystroke sequences. For example, if the Processor reads a B before an S, it knows the S must stand for Start Backup since it followed the Backup menu selection. Similarly, if the sequence were R, S, the Processor would interpret the S to mean Start Restore.

Using the first-letter codes, let's see what a batch file for a full backup—using the FASTBACK PLUS default settings—might look like:

**BSES**

This would stand for:

    Backup—Select the Backup menu
    Start Backup—Select the Backup Progress menu
    Estimate—Estimate the time and number of disks for this backup
    Start Backup—Start the backup

All the right menu selections are there, and the context tells the Macro Command Processor how to interpret them. But it still isn't quite complete, because when you select these items from the menu, you press ENTER each time. The ENTER keystrokes need to be represented in the batch file just like any other keystroke.

The ENTER key is represented in the Macro Command Language by the ) character. Thus, the correct sequence for our full backup is:

**B)S)E)S)**

Of course, other non-character keys have to be represented in the Macro Command Language as well. Function keys, Arrow keys, editing keys— all have their representation in the FASTBACK PLUS Macro Command Language. Tables 12-1 through 12-4 summarize the various groups of non-character keys and their representations in the Macro Command Language.

### Function Keys

Function keys are represented by an = sign followed by the number of the function key. Table 12-1 summarizes the FASTBACK PLUS function keys.

*Table 12-1: FASTBACK PLUS Function Keys*

| Key | Represented By | Function |
| --- | --- | --- |
| F1 | =1 | Get Context-Sensitive Help Screens. |
| F2 | =2 | Get Current Settings Summary. |
| F3 | =3 | Get Directory Tree. |
| F6 | =6 | MS-DOS Command. |
| F7 | =7 | Keystrokes to File. |
| F8 | =8 | Playback Keystrokes. |
| F9 | =9 | Load Setup File. |
| F10 | =10 | Save Setup File. |

## Movement Keys

The keys that allow you to move around and scroll through menus are located on your computer's numeric keypad and are generally represented by a slash character (/) followed by the number that appears on the key you want to represent. Note one exception to this rule—the TAB key allows you to move between windows in a directory tree and between fields in the Choose Files to Include/Exclude window, but since it is not located on the numeric keypad, it can't be represented with the "/numeral" code of the other movement keys. Instead, the TAB key is represented with the ( character. Table 12-2 summarizes the movement keys.

*Table 12-2: FASTBACK PLUS Movement Keys*

| Key | Represented By | Function |
| --- | --- | --- |
| UP ARROW | /8 | Move highlight bar up to previous menu item |
| DOWN ARROW | /2 | Move highlight bar down to next menu item |
| LEFT ARROW | /4 | Move highlight bar back to previous menu |
| RIGHT ARROW | /6 | Move highlight bar forward to next menu |
| PG UP | /9 | Scroll up one screen in current window |
| PG DN | /3 | Scroll down one screen in current window |
| HOME | /7 | Go to beginning of current window |
| END | /1 | Go to end of current window |
| TAB | ( | Jump between windows in the Directory Tree screen or to next field in the Choose Files window. |

## Editing Keys

The keys you use to edit entries when you are selecting files in FASTBACK PLUS, each have their own special representation. Table 12-3 summarizes the editing keys.

*Table 12-3: FASTBACK PLUS Editing Keys*

| Key | Represented By | Function |
| --- | --- | --- |
| INS | /I | Copy the highlighted file or directory from a directory tree into the Choose Files window. |

| Key | Represented By | Function |
|---|---|---|
| DEL | /D | Delete the current character in a pathname entry. |
| BACKSPACE | /L | Delete the previous character in a pathname entry. |
| CTRL-BACKSPACE | /B | Delete entire pathname entry. |
| ESC | $ | Leave current menu/window and return to previous menu/window. |
| ENTER | ) | Confirm currently highlighted menu choice or typed pathname. |

### Non-Keystroke Codes

In addition to recording the actual keystrokes you want executed in a batch file, you need to be able to signal FASTBACK PLUS to do certain procedure management tasks when necessary. For example, it is a good idea to tell FASTBACK PLUS how you want it to handle processing errors it might encounter while executing your batch file. The Macro Command Language includes a set of non-keystroke codes for this purpose. Table 12-4 summarizes the non-keystroke codes.

*Table 12-4: FASTBACK PLUS Non-keystroke Codes*

| Code | Instruction To Fastback Plus | Comments |
|---|---|---|
| @ | /Delimit command filename in a DOS command line | Can be used in a direct DOS command line entry or in a DOS batch file that includes a FASTBACK PLUS batch file name. For example, @EXKEY or @EXKEY@ calls our example keystroke macro file from Chapter 11, EXKEY.FB. |

| Code | Instruction To Fastback Plus | Comments |
|------|------------------------------|----------|
| %1 | Accept user input in a DOS batch file | This is a DOS *replaceable parameter*, not actually a FASTBACK PLUS code. Use this code—in DOS batch files only—to accept input from the user. For example, this code is included in the FASTBACK PLUS sample DOS batch files (included on the master diskette and discussed later in this chapter) to allow the user to type the letter of the hard disk to be backed up or restored. |
| ~ | Delay execution of the next keystroke for one second | Use this code when you want to slow a keystroke playback down for better viewing. |
| ' | Pause execution of batch file and wait for the user to press any key to continue execution | Use this code when you want to allow yourself (or other users) time to do something in the midst of a batch file. FASTBACK PLUS prompts the user to "Press SPACE BAR to continue, or Press ESC to abort." |
| { } | Send any text inside these braces to the screen | You can include on-screen messages to users in a batch file by enclosing the message text in braces. |
| " " | Take everything between this and the next quote as literal text | Use quotes (" ") to surround actual filenames (that is, not the name of your batch file), wildcard strings, etc. within a batch file, otherwise FASTBACK PLUS will interpret each keystroke separately as a batch file command. |
| [ ] | For any commands enclosed in brackets, conceal the attending menus and screens unless they are progress menus or menus that require user input. | Use the [ ] codes to turn FASTBACK PLUS's Invisible Mode on and off, thus eliminating a lot of the screen flashing that can occur during macro playback |

| Code | Instruction To Fastback Plus | Comments |
|------|------------------------------|----------|
| # | In case of processing error, continue executing batch file as well as possible | Related to DOS batch file error checking. |
| ^ | In case of processing error, discontinue executing batch file and return control to the keyboard | Related to DOS batch file error checking. |
| ! | In case of processing error, abort current operation and exit to DOS | Related to DOS batch file error checking. |
| & | Sound a beep tone | Use this code at the end of a batch file backup procedure to signal a completed backup when backing up files onto a large-capacity device. |

## Running FASTBACK PLUS Procedures from DOS

To start up FASTBACK PLUS, you type a startup command, FB, at the DOS command line prompt (usually C:>). You can also execute FAST-BACK PLUS macro commands from DOS, in three ways:

- Include the filename of a FASTBACK PLUS batch file on the DOS command line when you type FB to start FASTBACK PLUS.
- Type macro commands in directly, following the FASTBACK PLUS startup command (FB).
- Include a batch filename or direct macro commands with the FASTBACK PLUS startup command in a DOS batch file; the FASTBACK PLUS commands will be executed along with any DOS commands when you execute the DOS batch file.

### Executing a FASTBACK PLUS Batch File From DOS

To execute a FASTBACK PLUS batch file from the DOS command line, you simply add it to the FASTBACK PLUS startup command. For example, suppose you want to use the EXKEY.FB macro file we created in Chapter 11 to change the colors of your FASTBACK PLUS screens and change the FASTBACK PLUS prompt sound each time you start up FASTBACK PLUS. At the DOS prompt, you would type:

```
C:>FB @EXKEY.FB
```

and then press ENTER.

Remember, the @ is necessary to tell FASTBACK PLUS that what follows is a macro filename and not macro commands themselves.

### Executing FASTBACK PLUS Macro Commands Directly from DOS

Executing FASTBACK PLUS macro commands directly from the DOS command line is similar to executing a macro file from DOS. You type FB to start FASTBACK PLUS, and then before pressing ENTER, you also type the macro commands you want to execute. For example, if you plan to make an immediate backup, you could instruct FASTBACK PLUS to start estimating the time and disks required at the same time you start the program up:

```
C:>FB S))
```

When you press ENTER, FASTBACK PLUS will start up (FB), go to the Backup Progress menu (S highlights Start Backup, and), for ENTER, selects it), and start the backup estimate (The macro command) selects Estimate because it is already highlighted as the initial position on the Backup Progress menu.

### Including FASTBACK PLUS Macro Command Lines in DOS Batch Files

If you use DOS batch (.BAT) files, you may want to include FASTBACK PLUS commands in them. This capability provides powerful automation for your backup routines.

For example, you could create a DOS batch file that started FASTBACK PLUS for you, executed an entire full backup routine, only prompting you for disks, and then exited back to DOS. All you would have to do is type the name of the DOS batch file and then switch disks when prompted. And if you have a large capacity storage device, you might not even have to switch disks.

Creating a DOS batch file is just as easy as creating a FASTBACK PLUS batch file. You simply type a series (or "batch") of DOS command lines, and save the file with a name that indicates its purpose, plus a file extension of .BAT. You can create DOS batch files with nothing but FAST-BACK PLUS commands in them. Or you can mix FASTBACK PLUS commands in with other DOS commands.

### Online Batch Files

You can create a DOS batch file *online*, or interactively, by following these steps:

**Step 1**    At the DOS prompt, type COPY CON: FILENAME.BAT, and press ENTER. Figure 12-1 illustrates this.

COPY CON: tells DOS to copy what you type at the *console*, which is the name DOS uses to refer to your keyboard. In other words, you are telling DOS to record your keystrokes.

**FILENAME.BAT** stands for the filename you choose for this batch file, with a DOS batch file extension of .BAT.

**Step 2**    Type the FASTBACK PLUS macro commands you want the batch file to execute.

*Figure 12-1: COPY CON: FILENAME.BAT*

```
The time is 13:26:39.24
Today's date is Wed 5-16-1990
C:\>COPY CON: EST.BAT
```

In Figure 12-2, we have used the sequence of commands we saw earlier for starting up FASTBACK PLUS and immediately beginning the backup estimate.

**Step 3**    Press CTRL-Z and then press ENTER.

*Figure 12-2: Sample FASTBACK PLUS Command Sequence*

```
C:\>
The time is 13:31:12.22
Today's date is Wed 5-16-1990

C:\>COPY CON: EST.BAT
FB S))^Z
        1 File(s) copied

The time is 13:31:41.00
Today's date is Wed 5-16-1990

C:\>
```

CTRL-Z (Hold down CTRL and press Z) signals DOS that the file is complete and you want to save it under the filename you gave.

Once you have completed these steps, you can run the batch file any time just by typing the filename (no need to type the extension, unless you have used a filename that you've used with other file extensions) and press ENTER.

### Offline Batch Files

You can also create a DOS batch file *offline*, that is, outside of DOS, by entering the commands in an ASCII text editor file and then saving the file for later use with the .BAT extension.

Remember—to include an existing FASTBACK PLUS batch file in a DOS command line, you must precede the filename with the @ character; otherwise, each character in the filename will be interpreted as a macro command and you'll most likely get into an error situation.

For example, you might create the following DOS batch file, called CUSTOM.FB to start up FASTBACK PLUS and then run EXKEY.FB to change the audible prompt and menu colors:

```
C:>
CD \FASTBACK
FB @EXKEY.FB
```

Note the @ before the filename EXKEY.FB.

### Sample DOS Batch Files

The master FASTBACK PLUS diskette contains two samples of DOS batch files that execute FASTBACK PLUS procedures: BACKUP.BAT and RESTORE.BAT.

BACKUP.BAT is designed to execute a full backup of any hard disk you designate. All you have to do is type at the DOS prompt:

```
BACKUP [Drive letter]
```

and press ENTER. For example, if you type:

```
BACKUP C
```

and press ENTER, DOS will read the BACKUP.BAT file and make a full backup of your C: drive. If you have a partition in D:, you would type:

BACKUP D

to make a full backup of the D: drive.

RESTORE.BAT works exactly the same way, except of course that it makes a full restore of your backup files to the designated hard disk.

Caution: do not try to use these sample DOS batch files while you are actually in FASTBACK PLUS. They only work from DOS.

### Including Messages to Users in Your Batch Files

FASTBACK PLUS allows you to communicate with users during execution of a batch file by embedding screen messages in the batch file. To do this, enclose the text of your message in braces: { }. When FASTBACK PLUS encounters the { symbol, it regards all text following to be screen message text until it reads the } symbol. FASTBACK PLUS sends the text in a message to the screen.

Important: to leave the message on the screen until the user presses a key, you must follow the } symbol with an apostrophe ('), which you may recall from Table 12-4, is the code that tells FASTBACK PLUS to pause and prompt the user to *Press SPACE BAR to continue or Press ESC to abort*. When FASTBACK PLUS detects a keystroke from the user, the screen message disappears and macro execution continues.

This screen message feature is handy for prompting users to do things like switch disks during a backup or restore procedure, or enter a filename.

### Making the FASTBACK PLUS Menus Invisible During Macro Execution

FASTBACK PLUS provides an *Invisible Mode* for macro execution, that can really improve the appearance of your macro procedures by eliminating a lot of the screen flashing as FASTBACK PLUS executes movement and selections through the menu system.

To conceal the attending menus of certain commands, enclose those commands in brackets: [ ].

The symbol [ turns Invisible Mode on: Precede the commands you wish to conceal with a [.

The symbol ] turns Invisible Mode off: Follow concealed commands with a ].

All menus for commands enclosed in brackets will be hidden unless they are progress menus or menus that require user input.

### Determining DOS Batch File Success

You can include the DOS ERRORLEVEL variable in a DOS batch file to determine if a backup or restore procedure succeeded or failed. Table 12-5 summarizes the ERRORLEVEL settings.

*Table 12-5: ERRORLEVEL Settings*

| Setting | Indication |
| --- | --- |
| 0 | No errors were detected. |
| 1 | An error warning was encountered, but execution was able to continue. |
| 2 | The user aborted execution by pressing ESC. |
| 3 | A fatal error was encountered and FASTBACK PLUS exited to DOS. |

Recall that FASTBACK PLUS provides codes to allow you to specify how to proceed, depending on the gravity of a given error. These codes were previously presented in Table 12-4.

# CHAPTER 13

# *More on the FASTBACK PLUS*
# *Advanced Options Menu*

In addition to the automating features of FASTBACK PLUS, several other advanced features are worth a closer look. This chapter provides a summary of information about four important selections available on the Experienced and Advanced Options menus:

- Data Compression
- Error Correction
- Password Protection
- MS-DOS Command

## Data Compression

**Compression of Data** from the Advanced Options menu, allows you to control the data compression mode that FASTBACK PLUS uses when it backs up your files. This is a very important feature to be aware of because it can save you lots of time and/or disk space, depending on which setting you choose. The Compression of Data feature is shown in Figure 13-1.

*Figure 13-1: Compression of Data on Advanced Options Menu*

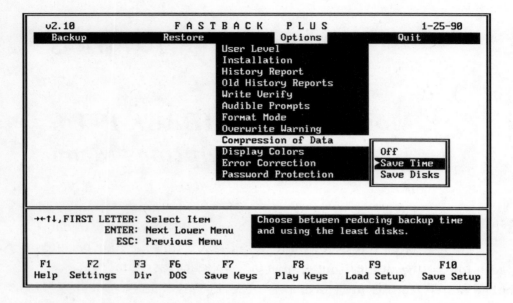

Compression of Data appears on the Advanced menu because it is such an important issue, not because it is difficult or complicated to use. Actually, it is quite easy to change the compression mode, and beginning FASTBACK PLUS users should feel free to do so. Here's how:

**Step 1**   Select **User Level** from the Beginner level Options menu.

A pop-up menu of user levels appears.

**Step 2**   Select **Advanced**.

The Options menu changes to reflect the greater variety of selections offered at the Advanced level.

**Step 3**   Now select **Compression of Data**.

Another pop-up menu appears, offering three compression alternatives. To help you make a decision about which mode to use, we can look at the advantages of each choice:

- **Off** Do not use data compression at all.

  This alternative is not recommended. Your backups will take maximum time and maximum floppy disk space if you don't use data compression, so you will only want to turn data compression off if you *really need* to have plain text on your backup disks.

- **Save Time** Use only idle processor time to do data compression.

  FASTBACK PLUS offers **Save Time** as the default data compression mode because it generally gives the broadest value—it offers enough compression so you save disk space, but not enough to cost you a lot of extra time. If you want to take advantage of data compression, but don't want to add extra time to your backup procedures, leave Compression of Data set at Save Time.

- **Save Disks** Do *maximum* data compression, using whatever time is necessary.

  Save Disks is by far the best choice if limiting the number of disks you use for a backup is significantly more important to you than saving a few minutes. Backing up your hard disk with data compression set to Save Disks can reduce the number of disks required to as much as half, although it is more common to save by more like a third.

  For example, in a recent full backup, FASTBACK PLUS estimated that the procedure would require 27 floppy disks with no data compression. With data compression set to Save Disks, however, the actual backup took 17 disks. The time estimated was 16:20, compared to an actual time of well over 20 minutes.

Note: when FASTBACK PLUS estimates the time and disks required for a backup, it does not consider the effect of data compression, even if you have it turned on. Thus, the disk estimate will always be the maximum number of disks the backup might take, and the time estimate may be greater or smaller, depending on the data compression mode you choose.

**Step 4** Select the Compression mode you want to use in your backup.

## Error Correction

One of FASTBACK PLUS's most important security features is its advanced error correction system. Depending on the circumstances, it allows FASTBACK PLUS to tolerate damage of up to 13 percent of a disk's surface and still recover the lost data. Figure 13-2 shows the Error Correction feature on the Advanced Options menu.

*Figure 13-2: Error Correction on Advanced Options Menu*

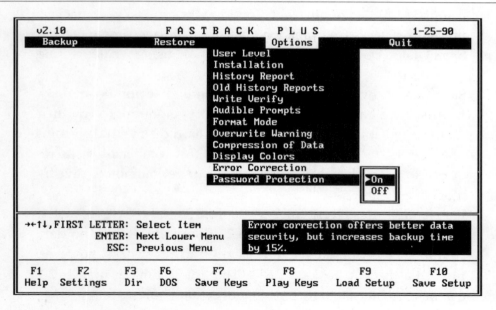

Because error correction is such an important feature for the security of your data, FASTBACK PLUS automatically sets it to On when you start the program. Every time you back up your files, FASTBACK PLUS writes extra error correction information to each floppy disk.

While turning error correction Off will reduce the time of your backups by about 15 percent, the few minutes you save can't compare to the amount of time and valuable data you stand to lose if something happens to damage your backup disks and you can't recover the lost data. Therefore, it is strongly recommended that you leave error correction turned On!

But in case you ever need to change this setting, here's how:

**Step 1**    Select **User Level** from the Beginner level Options menu.

A pop-up menu of user levels appears.

**Step 2**    Select **Advanced**.

The Options menu changes to reflect the greater variety of selections offered at the Advanced level.

**Step 3**    Now select **Error Correction**.

Another pop-up menu appears, offering the two possible Error Correction settings:

- **On**  Write error correction information to each backup disk so that if the disk is later damaged, FASTBACK PLUS can try to recover missing data.
- **Off**  Do not write error correction information to backup disks.

## Password Protection

Password protection is a new feature of FASTBACK PLUS. It was added to provide greater security to people whose computer system is accessible to others. Figure 13-3 shows the Password Protection feature on the Advanced Options menu.

*Figure 13-3: Password Protection on Advanced Options Menu*

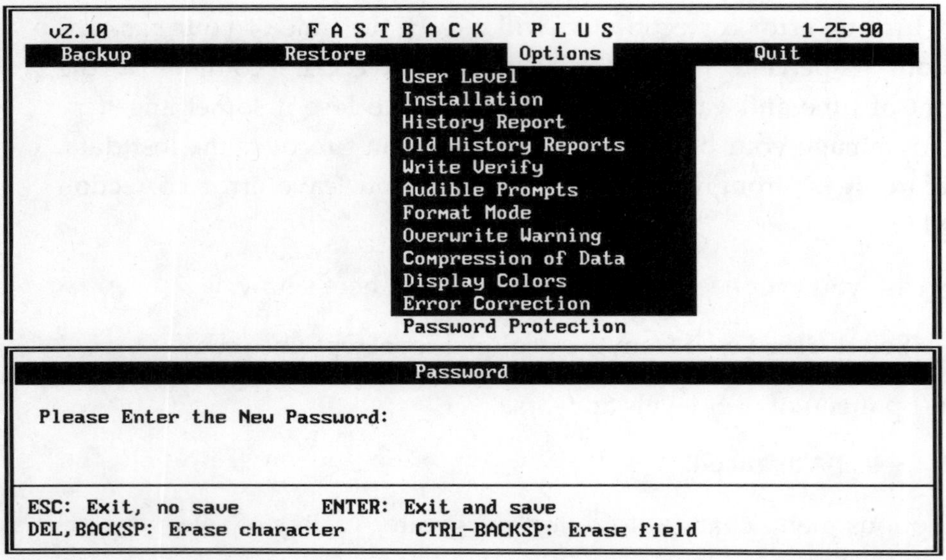

```
 v2.10              F A S T B A C K   P L U S           1-25-90
  Backup            Restore          Options              Quit
                                 User Level
                                 Installation
                                 History Report
                                 Old History Reports
                                 Write Verify
                                 Audible Prompts
                                 Format Mode
                                 Overwrite Warning
                                 Compression of Data
                                 Display Colors
                                 Error Correction
                                 Password Protection

                              Password

     Please Enter the New Password:



     ESC: Exit, no save       ENTER: Exit and save
     DEL,BACKSP: Erase character    CTRL-BACKSP: Erase field
```

The password protection scheme is simple, but powerful. It is simple because all you have to do to protect your backup files from unauthorized restoration is assign a simple password of your own choosing to the backup set. It is powerful because you run the risk of losing your own ability to restore your files if you forget your password!

This warning cannot be stressed enough: there is *no way* to restore password protected backup files if you enter an incorrect password or fail to enter a password at all!

If you need to protect your backup files from unauthorized use by others, select a password prior to starting the backup procedure. Here's how:

**Step 1**   Select **User Level** from the Beginner level Options menu.

A pop-up menu of user levels appears.

**Step 2**   Select **Advanced**.

The Options menu changes to reflect the greater variety of selections offered at the Advanced level.

**Step 3**   Now select **Password Protection**.

FASTBACK PLUS prompts you to enter a password.

**Step 4**   Type the password and then press ENTER.

Choose your password carefully. It can contain up to 40 characters with no spaces.

Warning: you *must* remember your password or you will not be able to restore your backups.

You see the password as you type it, but when you press ENTER, the password disappears.

When you press ENTER after typing your password, FASTBACK PLUS prompts you to enter it again for confirmation.

**Step 5**   Type your password once more and press ENTER.

**Step 6**   Proceed with your backup.

The files in this backup set will only be accessible to users who are able to enter the correct password before trying to restore them.

To restore a password-protected backup set, you use a procedure very similar to the one described above for assigning the password in the first place:

**Step 1**   Select the **Password Protection** option from the Advanced Options menu (changing the user level to Advanced first, if necessary).

**Step 2**   Then enter and confirm the correct password, following FASTBACK PLUS's prompts to do so.

**Step 3**   Proceed with your restore procedure. If you entered the correct password for the backup set, the restore proceeds as usual.

But if you entered an incorrect password or no password at all, FAST-BACK PLUS responds to your restore attempt with a Password Mismatch error.

Note that if you unwittingly enter the wrong password you won't realize it until FASTBACK PLUS halts the restore procedure with an error message. However, if you catch yourself in a typing mistake while entering the password, you can press SPACE and FASTBACK PLUS will let you try again.

If you can't remember the password for the backup set you want, you can press ESC to abort and skip doing the restore until you have remembered the correct password.

## MS-DOS Command (F6)

The Experienced level Options menu offers a handy feature: **MS-DOS Command**. This selection temporarily suspends FASTBACK PLUS so that you can issue one or more commands at the DOS prompt. Figure 13-4 shows the MS-DOS Command feature on the Experienced Options menu.

In addition to selecting it from the Experienced level Options menu, you can also activate the MS-DOS Command feature by pressing the F6 key. (In fact, at the Beginner and Advanced levels, this is the only way you can activate this feature.)

The MS-DOS Command can be very useful when you suddenly realize that you need to do something like change the default directory before beginning a restore procedure, or check the content of a certain file before deciding whether to include it in a backup.

*Figure 13-4: MS-DOS Command from Experienced Options Menu*

```
 Calling MS-DOS.  Type "EXIT<Enter>" to return to FASTBACK PLUS.
 SPERRY Personal Computer
 MS-DOS 3.10 version 1.15
 (C)Copyright Microsoft Corp 1981, 1985

 Command v. 3.10


 The time is  5:44:19.51
 Today's date is Thu  5-10-1990

 C:\WP\KATE\FBPIX>
```

Here is how to suspend FASTBACK PLUS operations so that you can perform necessary DOS tasks without actually leaving FASTBACK PLUS:

**Step 1**    Either select **MS-DOS Command** from the Experienced Options menu

or,

Press F6 from any level in FASTBACK PLUS.

The DOS prompt appears, replacing the FASTBACK PLUS screen that you were in.

**Step 2**    Enter and execute as many DOS commands as you like before returning to FASTBACK PLUS.

Warning: FASTBACK PLUS will still be resident in memory while you use the MS-DOS Command feature, so you will have less memory available in DOS. If DOS complains of insufficient memory, you will have to return to FASTBACK PLUS and select **Quit** from the Main menu before entering your DOS commands.

**Step 3**    When you are finished with DOS, type EXIT and press ENTER to return to FASTBACK PLUS.

Warning: you cannot use MS-DOS Command to interrupt an actual FASTBACK PLUS backup or restore procedure. If you need to interrupt a backup or restore procedure to do something in DOS, you will have to:

1. Press ESC to halt the procedure.
2. Use the MS-DOS Command feature and return to FASTBACK PLUS.
3. Restart the halted procedure from the beginning.

# *Installing FASTBACK PLUS*

## What You Should Know About Your Computer

You may have more than one hard disk on your computer, in addition to one or more floppy disk drives, and even tape drives. And they may all be different sizes and capacities. Before you install FASTBACK PLUS, you should make a point of determining exactly what your drive configuration is: the number and types of each hard disk, floppy drive, and tape drive you have.

This is important for two reasons:

1. Knowing the total capacity of your hard disk(s) will allow you to select the correct number of buffers when FASTBACK PLUS changes your CONFIG.SYS file during the installation, and it will also help you determine how many floppy disks you should have on hand for a full backup.

2. FASTBACK PLUS needs to make a record of the types of floppy drives you have during the installation procedure. You don't want to have to stop in the middle of installing FASTBACK PLUS to figure out what the exact size and capacity of your B drive is, so it is

best to gather the information now and have it in front of you before you start to install FASTBACK PLUS.

Filling out the following form will give you a record of your drive configuration:

### Hard Disks

**Main hard disk:**

Drive designation _____

Disk capacity _____

**Supplementary hard disks:**

Drive designation _____

Disk capacity _____

Drive designation _____

Disk capacity _____

### Floppy Drives:

**Drive A:**

Disk Type _____

**Drive B:**

Disk Type _____

If you don't know what disk type your floppy drives take, consult Table A-1, at the end of this section.

**Supplementary Drives:**

Designation _____

Disk Type _____

### Network Drives:

Pathname 1 _____

Type _____

Capacity _____

Pathname 2 _____

Type _____

Capacity _____

### Network Security?

The highest security level is required to make full backup of a network hard disk. If you are at a lower security level, FASTBACK PLUS will report an error upon encountering a protected file or directory.

Highest Level _____

### Other External Drives:

Pathname _____

Type _____

Capacity _____

Table A-1 summarizes the most common floppy drive configurations for several standard personal computer systems.

*Table A-1: Common Floppy Drive Configurations*

| System (and Compatibles) | Drive A: | Drive B: |
|---|---|---|
| IBM PC/One drive | 40 track 5.25 inch (360k) | |
| IBM PC/Two drives | 40 track 5.25 inch (360k) | 40 track 5.25 inch (360k) |
| IBM PC/AT | 80 track 5.25 high density (1.2 mb) | 40 track 5.25 inch (360k) |
| IBM PS/2 Mod. 30 | 80 track 3.5 inch (730k) | |

| *System (and Compatibles)* | *Drive A:* | *Drive B:* |
|---|---|---|
| IBM PS/2 Mod. 50 | 80 track 3.5 inch (1.44 mb) | |
| IBM PS/2 Mod. 80 | 80 track 3.5 inch (1.44 mb) | |
| TOSHIBA 3100 | 80 track 3.5 inch (730k) | |

## The Installation Procedures

Installing FASTBACK PLUS involves five brief procedures:

- Making a copy of the FASTBACK PLUS master diskette.
- Copying the files on the FASTBACK PLUS master diskette (referred to as the distribution diskette) to a directory on your hard disk.
- Defining your system's floppy drive configuration for FASTBACK PLUS.
- Having FASTBACK PLUS make some minor changes to your AUTOEXEC.BAT and CONFIG.SYS files that will help you get the most efficient use of FASTBACK PLUS.
- Running a speed test on your hardware and a Backup/Restore Confidence test to ensure that FASTBACK PLUS is working properly after you've installed it.

Except for making a copy of the FASTBACK PLUS master diskette for safe keeping, FASTBACK PLUS actually does all the rest of the installation itself. You just answer a few on-screen questions about the configuration of your system.

The following sections outline the steps required to complete each of the five FASTBACK PLUS installation procedures. When you have completed these procedures, you will be ready to use FASTBACK PLUS.

If you have not already done so, take a moment now to fill out the relevant parts of the form provided in the previous section to describe your computer's configuration. You will want to have some of this information available during Procedure 3, and some of it—for example the information about security on network drives if your computer is networked to other systems on a Local Area Network—may come in handy later on.

### Installation Procedure 1: Make a Copy of the Master Diskette

It is very important to make a copy of the FASTBACK PLUS master diskette before proceeding with the installation. If something goes wrong during the installation, you will have a complete copy of FASTBACK PLUS to work with.

It is a good idea, actually, to use your *copy* of FASTBACK PLUS for the installation and put the actual master diskette away for safekeeping.

**Step 1**   With the DOS prompt (usually, C:\) on the screen, place a blank or reusable disk in drive A and type:

```
FORMAT A:
```

You cannot copy FASTBACK PLUS onto an unformatted floppy disk. If you are reusing an old disk, formatting it will erase its contents.

When DOS finishes formatting this disk, it will ask you if you want to format another. Answer N for No.

**Step 2**   Place the FASTBACK PLUS master diskette in drive A and the formatted disk in drive B.

If you only have an A drive, you will have to disk-swap at the appropriate times. DOS will prompt you to swap disks when necessary.

**Step 3**   Type:

```
DISKCOPY A: B:
```

and press ENTER.

Note: for a single drive, type DISKCOPY A: A:.

DOS prompts you to confirm that the correct disks are in the correct drives.

**Step 4**   Press ENTER to confirm disk placement.

DOS will inform you when the copying process is complete.

**Step 5**   Remove both disks and put one away for safekeeping.

### Installation Procedure 2: Copying FASTBACK PLUS Files to Your Hard Disk

FASTBACK PLUS normally runs from your hard disk, so you must copy all of its files onto the hard disk. FASTBACK PLUS provides a batch file, FBINSTAL.BAT to do this for you. All you have to do is place the master diskette in drive A and call FBINSTAL.

**Step 1**   Place the FASTBACK PLUS master diskette (or your copy) in Drive A.

**Step 2**   Type:

```
A:
```

and press ENTER to change the default drive to A.

The DOS prompt should now be A:\, as shown in Figure A-1.

*Figure A-1: The A:>\ Prompt*

```
The time is 16:27:28.40
Today's date is Thus 5-17-1990

A:\>
```

**Step 3**   Type:

```
FBINSTAL
```

and press ENTER to run the FBINSTAL.BAT program, as shown in Figure A-2.

*Figure A-2: Type FBINSTAL and Press ENTER*

```
The time is 16:27:28.40
Today's date is Thu 5-17-1990

A:\>FBINSTAL
```

*Figure A-3: Prompt for Installation Drive and Directory*

```
 v2.10          F A S T B A C K   P L U S   I N S T A L L     1-25-90
┌──────────────────────────────────────────────────────────────────┐
│                            W E L C O M E                           │
│                                                                    │
│ Welcome!  This program will quickly install Fastback Plus to perform│
│ properly with your computer's hardware.  The install procedure consists of│
│ the following steps:                                               │
│                                                                    │
│ 1. Copy the distribution files.                                    │
│ 2. Change AUTOEXEC.BAT to support Fastback Plus.                   │
│ 3. Change the "BUFFERS =" statement in CONFIG.SYS.                 │
│ 4. State which floppy drives you plan to use.                      │
│                                                                    │
│ You will be able to skip steps 1 through 3 if you wish.  You may abort this│
│ install program any time by pressing <Escape>.                     │
│                                                                    │
│ Name the drive and path on which to install                        │
│ Fastback Plus, or press <Enter> for  C:\FASTBACK.                  │
│                                                                    │
│                                                                    │
│                                                                    │
└──────────────────────────────────────────────────────────────────┘
```

FASTBACK PLUS prompts you to enter the name of the drive and directory where you want to install FASTBACK PLUS, as shown in Figure A-3. The default is C:\FASTBACK.

**Step 4**   Press ENTER to accept the default drive and directory, or type in the drive and directory you prefer, and then press ENTER.

If you enter a different drive and directory, the format should be:

```
L:\DIRECTORY
```

where L stands for the drive designation letter and DIRECTORY is the directory name.

FASTBACK PLUS displays a Copy Files screen, which presents a series of prompts related to copying the FASTBACK PLUS files from the distribution diskette (the FASTBACK PLUS master diskette) to your designated drive and directory.

**Step 5**   Answer the prompts as follows:

Prompt 1: *Do you wish to copy the files from the distribution diskette? (Y or N).* Answer Y. This prompt is shown in Figure A-4.

*Figure A-4: The First Prompt*

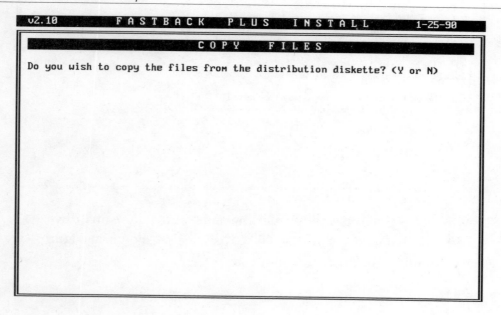

Prompt 2: *Name the drive containing the distribution diskette? (A through P)*. Answer A, unless you plan to insert the distribution diskette in some other drive. This prompt is shown in Figure A-5.

*Figure A-5: The Second Prompt*

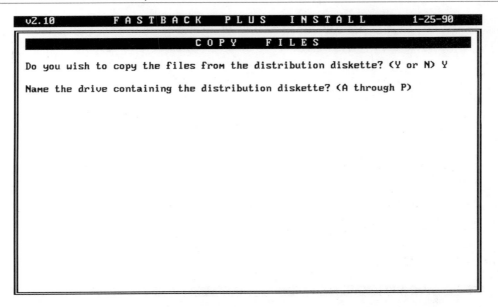

Prompt 3: *You will be copying from drive A: to drive C: Correct? (Y or N)*. Answer Y. This prompt is shown in Figure A-6.

**Step 6**  If you haven't already done so, insert the distribution diskette in drive A: and press ENTER to start the copying procedure. FASTBACK PLUS will prompt you for the disk, as shown in Figure A-7.

When all the FASTBACK PLUS files have been copied into the designated directory on your hard drive, the screen changes to prompt you through the next procedure, as shown in Figure A-8.

*Figure A-6: The Third Prompt*

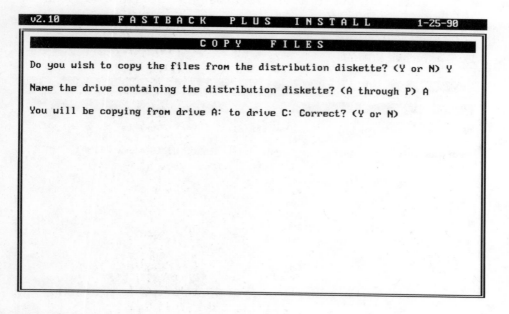

*Figure A-7: FASTBACK PLUS Prompts for the Disk*

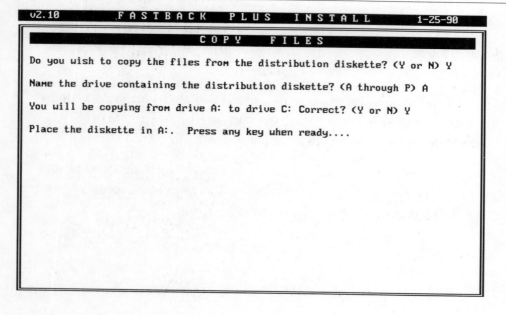

*Figure A-8: All Files Have Been Copied to Your Hard Disk*

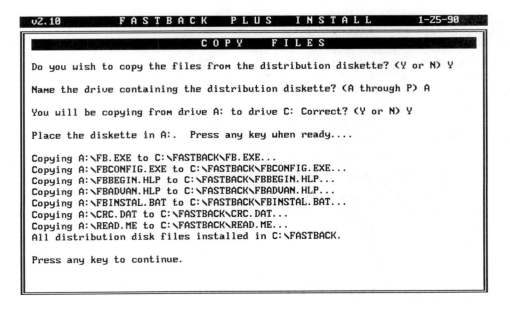

```
v2.10        F A S T B A C K   P L U S   I N S T A L L        1-25-90

                        C O P Y     F I L E S

Do you wish to copy the files from the distribution diskette? (Y or N) Y

Name the drive containing the distribution diskette? (A through P) A

You will be copying from drive A: to drive C: Correct? (Y or N) Y

Place the diskette in A:.  Press any key when ready....

Copying A:\FB.EXE to C:\FASTBACK\FB.EXE...
Copying A:\FBCONFIG.EXE to C:\FASTBACK\FBCONFIG.EXE...
Copying A:\FBBEGIN.HLP to C:\FASTBACK\FBBEGIN.HLP...
Copying A:\FBADVAN.HLP to C:\FASTBACK\FBADVAN.HLP...
Copying A:\FBINSTAL.BAT to C:\FASTBACK\FBINSTAL.BAT...
Copying A:\CRC.DAT to C:\FASTBACK\CRC.DAT...
Copying A:\READ.ME to C:\FASTBACK\READ.ME...
All distribution disk files installed in C:\FASTBACK.

Press any key to continue.
```

## Installation Procedure 3: Changing AUTOEXEC.BAT and CONFIG.SYS

After you have copied the FASTBACK PLUS files to your hard disk, FASTBACK PLUS offers to change your CONFIG.SYS and AU-TOEXEC.BAT files to allow more efficient use of FASTBACK PLUS.

The change to AUTOEXEC.BAT adds a PATH command that lets you run FASTBACK PLUS from any directory, rather than having to first change to the \FASTBACK directory.

The change to CONFIG.SYS adds a command to match the number of buffers (active work areas used in copying files to or from a disk) to the size of your hard disk. If you have no CONFIG.SYS, FASTBACK PLUS creates one. This addition to the CONFIG.SYS makes FASTBACK PLUS's backup performance more efficient.

You don't have to do anything but answer the prompt for each of these changes. FASTBACK PLUS changes the files automatically.

**Step 1**   Answer Y to the prompt for changing your AUTOEXEC.BAT file.
Figure A-9 shows what your screen will look like.

*Figure A-9: FASTBACK PLUS Explains Change to AUTOEXEC.BAT*

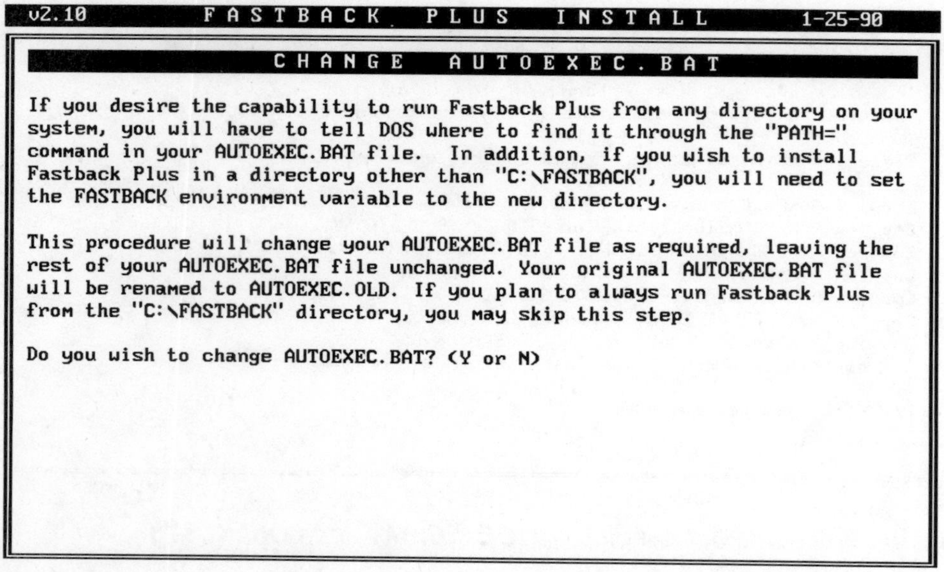

```
 v2.10          F A S T B A C K   P L U S   I N S T A L L          1-25-90
┌──────────────────────────────────────────────────────────────────────┐
│                    C H A N G E    A U T O E X E C . B A T              │
│                                                                        │
│   If you desire the capability to run Fastback Plus from any directory on your │
│   system, you will have to tell DOS where to find it through the "PATH=" │
│   command in your AUTOEXEC.BAT file.  In addition, if you wish to install │
│   Fastback Plus in a directory other than "C:\FASTBACK", you will need to set │
│   the FASTBACK environment variable to the new directory.              │
│                                                                        │
│   This procedure will change your AUTOEXEC.BAT file as required, leaving the │
│   rest of your AUTOEXEC.BAT file unchanged. Your original AUTOEXEC.BAT file │
│   will be renamed to AUTOEXEC.OLD. If you plan to always run Fastback Plus │
│   from the "C:\FASTBACK" directory, you may skip this step.            │
│                                                                        │
│   Do you wish to change AUTOEXEC.BAT? (Y or N)                         │
│                                                                        │
└──────────────────────────────────────────────────────────────────────┘
```

**Step 2**   Answer Y to the prompt for changing your CONFIG.SYS file.
Figure A-10 shows what your screen will look like.

**Step 3**   FASTBACK PLUS displays a list of recommended buffer values
for you to choose from on the basis of the size of your hard disk, as
shown in Figure A-11.

Enter the number that corresponds to the size of your hard disk.

When both files have been changed, FASTBACK PLUS goes on to the
next installation procedure, defining your floppy drives.

*Figure A-10: FASTBACK PLUS Explains Change to CONFIG.SYS*

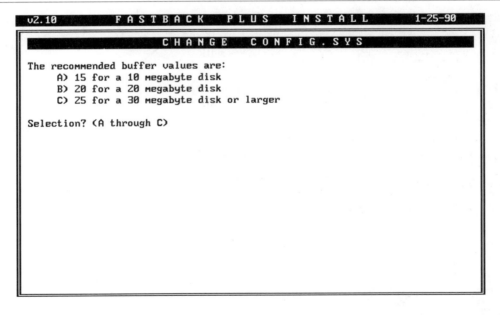

```
v2.10          F A S T B A C K   P L U S   I N S T A L L      1-25-90

                    C H A N G E   C O N F I G . S Y S

To obtain the best hard disk performance from DOS the "BUFFERS =" command in
your CONFIG.SYS file needs to be set to match the capacity of your hard
disk.   This will not only optimize performance while using Fastback Plus,
but also give you best performance when using other application programs.
There is no hard and fast rule for selecting which DOS buffer size works
best for your computer, but the settings recommended below will give you
better performance than using the DOS default value.  If you are using a
disk caching program, you will probably want to skip this procedure. This
procedure will change the number of buffers used, leaving the rest of
CONFIG.SYS unchanged.   Your original CONFIG.SYS file will be renamed to
CONFIG.OLD.

Do you wish to change CONFIG.SYS? (Y or N)
```

*Figure A-11: Recommended Buffer Values for CONFIG.SYS*

```
v2.10          F A S T B A C K   P L U S   I N S T A L L      1-25-90

                    C H A N G E   C O N F I G . S Y S

The recommended buffer values are:
      A) 15 for a 10 megabyte disk
      B) 20 for a 20 megabyte disk
      C) 25 for a 30 megabyte disk or larger

Selection? (A through C)
```

### Installation Procedure 4: Defining Your Floppy Drives

In order to perform backup and restore operations on your files, FAST-BACK PLUS needs to know exactly what type of disk is used by each of your floppy drives.

You give the program this information by selecting the correct drive definition for each of your drives from a list presented on the **Define Floppy Drives** screen. FASTBACK PLUS prompts you to enter a selection for each of your drives.

Note: if you're not sure what kind of floppy drives your system has, check Table A-1 in the preceding section. The most common personal computer systems and their standard drive configurations are listed there. If you don't find your computer or one that is compatible with (many brands of computers are compatible with one of the IBM models of personal computers, which means they are built to run the same software, and usually have the same drive configurations as similar model IBM systems) your computer in Table A-1, check the documentation that came with your computer for information about its drive configuration.

**Step 1**   FASTBACK PLUS will prompt you for the A drive definition, as shown in Figure A-12. Enter the number of the correct definition for your A drive from the list on the screen.

FASTBACK PLUS now prompts you to define your B: drive, as shown in Figure A-13.

**Step 2**   Enter the number of the correct definition for your B drive from the list on the screen. If you do not have a B: drive, enter **6**.

FASTBACK PLUS displays the definitions you have selected for each drive and prompts you to confirm your choices, as shown in Figure A-14.

**Step 3**   Answer Y to confirm your drive definitions.

*Figure A-12: Prompt for the A Drive Definition*

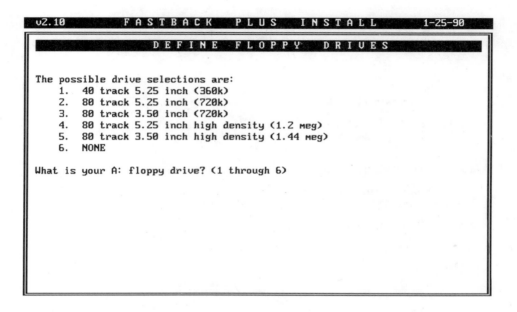

*Figure A-13: Prompt for the B: Drive Definition*

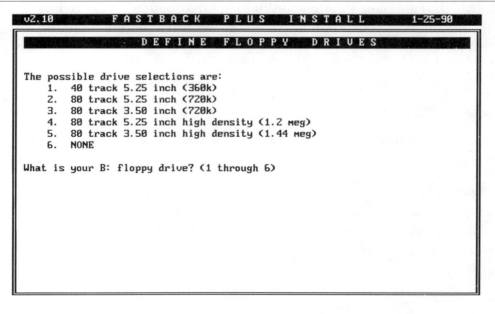

*Figure A-14: Confirming Your Drive Definitions*

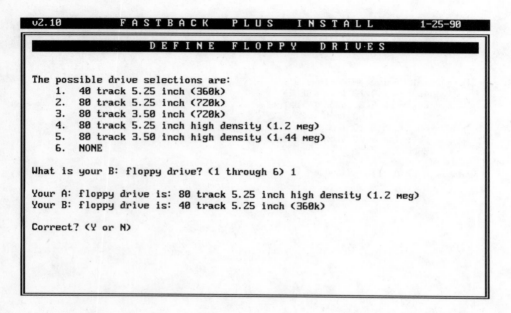

Note: if one of the definitions is incorrect, answer N. FASTBACK PLUS will then prompt you through the floppy drive definition procedure again.

Completion of your drive definitions brings you to the fifth and final installation procedure, running the hardware tests.

### Installation Procedure 5: Hardware Testing

Before you can use FASTBACK PLUS, the program needs to run two tests on your equipment:

**The Hardware Test**   This test determines the accessibility of your Direct Memory Access controller chip. This is critical because FASTBACK PLUS achieves its tremendous speed by making use of Direct Memory Access to read files from one disk and write to another at the same time. In doing this, FASTBACK PLUS uses all four of your DMA channels.

The hardware test determines your computer's read and write performance at three different speeds: low, medium, and high.

**The Backup/Restore Confidence Test**  backs up selected data from your hard disk and then compares the backup version with the original version. This test is just a check to make sure FASTBACK PLUS is working smoothly with your system.

If your system passes all three hardware speed tests, FASTBACK PLUS performs the Backup/Restore Confidence Test automatically, and you won't have to do anything further. But if it fails the hardware tests, you will have to reboot (press CTRL-ALT-DEL) and follow the procedures outlined at the end of this section to set the DMA speed and run the Backup/Restore Confidence test manually.

Don't be alarmed when you see an error message and perhaps some erratic behavior from DOS after a hardware test failure. Just reboot.

After you complete the definition of your floppy drives, FASTBACK PLUS presents a screen that explains the tests it is about to do. This screen prompts you to *Press any key to continue...*

**Step 1**  Press ENTER to proceed to the Hardware Test.

FASTBACK PLUS actually starts itself now, immediately taking you past the Main menu to the **Test Hardware** selection under Installation on the Options menu.

Here, it prompts you to enter a disk of an appropriate type in your A: drive, as shown in Figure A-15.

Warning: the disk you use for this hardware test will be overwritten—be sure to insert a disk that you don't mind having overwritten!

**Step 2**  Insert a blank or reusable disk in drive A and press ENTER. FASTBACK PLUS now performs the three speed tests, reporting on each one as it is completed.

*Figure A-15: FASTBACK PLUS Prompts You for a Blank Disk*

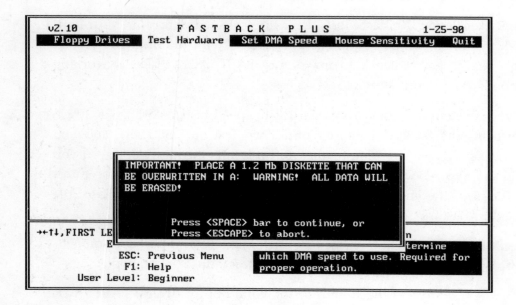

When the speed tests are completed—assuming your computer passed all three—FASTBACK PLUS immediately starts itself and begins to perform the Backup/Restore Confidence test. This is illustrated in Figure A-16.

When that test is completed, FASTBACK PLUS notifies you that you have successfully completed the installation process, and returns control to DOS. Figure A-17 shows a successful installation.

**Setting the DMA Speed Manually**   If your computer failed one or more of the three speed tests described earlier in this section, you will have to reboot and set the DMA speed yourself before you use FASTBACK PLUS. To do this:

**Step 1**   Press CTRL-ALT-DEL to reboot your computer.

**Step 2**   Type FB and press ENTER to start up FASTBACK PLUS.

*Figure A-16: FASTBACK PLUS Starts Itself for Confidence Test*

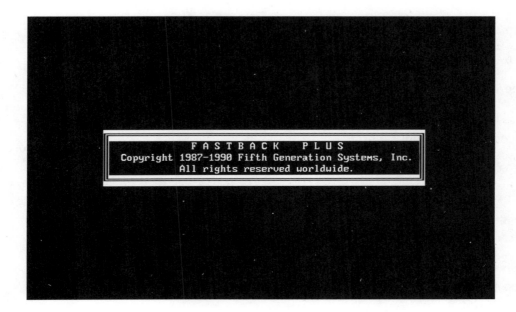

*Figure A-17: A Successful Installation*

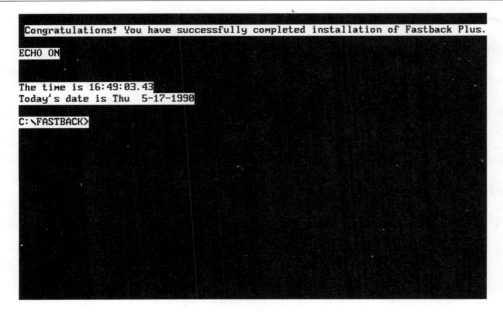

You will start out at FASTBACK PLUS's opening menu, the Backup menu.

**Step 3**   Press the RIGHT ARROW key until you reach the Options menu.

**Step 4**   Press **I** and then ENTER to select the Installation menu.

**Step 5**   Press **S** and then ENTER to select Set DMA Speed.

The highlight bar is on the highest speed your computer passed in the speed tests. Leave it there.

**Step 6**   Press ENTER to set your DMA speed to the highlighted speed.

Caution: if you manually set your DMA speed higher than the highest speed your computer passed in the hardware test, you run the risk of corrupting your data, or losing it altogether. You may set it to a lower speed if you wish.

**Step 7**   Press ESC to return to the Options menu.

**Running the Backup/Restore Confidence Test Manually**   After you have set the DMA speed, you can perform your own Backup/Restore Confidence test with the following steps:

**Step 1**   Move back to the Backup Menu from the Options menu.

**Step 2**   Select Choose Files.

**Step 3**   At the highlighted place in the Choose Files to Include window, type \FASTBACK.

**Step 4**   Press ESC to return to the Backup menu.

**Step 5**   Select Start Backup from the Backup menu.

**Step 6**   Select Start Backup from the Backup Progress menu.

**Step 7**   Follow the screen prompts for disk insertion during the backup.

(Backing up the \FASTBACK directory alone should take no more than one disk.)

**Step 8**   When the backup is completed, select Quit to return to the Main menu.

**Step 9**   Move to the Restore menu and select Start Restore.

**Step 10**   Select Compare Files from the Restore Progress menu.

If the files on the disk in your A drive match the files in the \FASTBACK directory on your hard disk, the backup worked correctly and you can use FASTBACK PLUS to back up other files on your hard disk with high confidence.

## Creating a Reboot Disk for Emergencies

In case of a hard disk crash, you should create a disk that will allow you to reboot your computer and perform a restore of your last full backup.

To do this:

**Step 1**   Insert a blank floppy disk into drive A: and type:

```
FORMAT A:/S
```

Then press ENTER.

**Step 2**   Copy your AUTOEXEC.BAT and CONFIG.SYS files and the contents of your \FASTBACK directory onto the floppy by typing these commands, pressing ENTER after each one:

```
COPY C:\AUTOEXEC.BAT A:
COPY C:\CONFIG.SYS A:
COPY C:\FASTBACK\*.* A:
```

If you should ever need to reboot and restore your latest backup because of a hard disk failure, you can place this disk in drive A: and then start your computer. At the A: prompt, type FB to start FASTBACK PLUS, and then follow the instructions in Chapter 8 of this book to perform a full restore of your latest backup set.

Store your Reboot/Restore disk in a safe place!

# *FASTBACK PLUS Error Messages*

This appendix lists all of the FASTBACK PLUS error messages in numerical order, offering clarification where needed and suggesting solutions or workarounds when possible. You may notice that gaps occur in the error message numbering sequence. Don't worry about it—FASTBACK PLUS's numeric classification system skips some numbers.

Some FASTBACK PLUS error messages are relatively innocuous. When a longer-than-expected delay in disk switching occurs, for example, Error 28 reports that FASTBACK PLUS is *Waiting for confirmation of disk switch*. In such cases, where no real hardware or software problem is involved, FASTBACK PLUS tells the user how to proceed from the error—usually with instructions to press ENTER to proceed once the expected task has been performed, or to press ESC if it is necessary to abort. These proceed instructions appear after the error, in the error message box.

In other cases, where there might actually be a hardware or software problem, but it is not serious enough to halt the current operation, FAST-BACK PLUS will issue a warning, but still allow the user to proceed from the error.

And of course, some errors indicate serious disk or software problems that will require repair or intervention of some kind. In these cases, FASTBACK PLUS may simply skip parts of the operation that cannot be completed under the error circumstances, halt the current operation, or, in the worst cases, crash.

Each serious error has its own set of possible solutions that must be described individually.

If no alternative solution is suggested either by FASTBACK PLUS or in this book, contact a service representative for your computer or the technical support staff at Fifth Generation Systems. You will find their telephone number in Chapter 7 of the FASTBACK PLUS User Manual that came with your software.

## Error Messages

### 1: Insufficient memory! Aborting.

The required 330k of memory is not available to FASTBACK PLUS. Try unloading memory resident programs such as desktop utilities, print spoolers, disk caches, etc. You can also try removing or reducing the size of your RAM disk if you use one.

### 2: Unable to open specified batch command file!

Either the pathname or the filename you entered is incorrect. Check your typing and try again.

### 3: Insufficient memory for this operation! Reduce memory resident programs and retry.

The setup file you are trying to load requires more memory than is available.

### 4: Unable to save setup information!

FASTBACK PLUS encountered a write error. The most likely problems are: An incorrect path or file name, or a full or write-protected diskette. Occasionally, this error indicates insufficient environment space to set the "FASTBACK=" variable in CONFIG.SYS.

### 5: Unable to find or create support directory!

Your hard disk may be too full to create the support directory for storing the FASTBACK PLUS files. Try removing unneeded files from your disk.

### 6: Drive is not available!

You may have mistyped the drive designation.

### 7: Operation interrupted! Processing is suspended.

FASTBACK PLUS responds with this message when you press ESC to interrupt an operation.

### 8: Printer not ready!

The printer may not be turned on, or may not be properly connected or installed.

### 9: Unable to create path [PATHNAME]. The path name conflicts with an existing file name! Confirm renaming the file extension to ".SAV".

When FASTBACK PLUS encounters a duplicated filename, it responds by changing the file extension of the file it is trying to create to .SAV. You must confirm this change.

### 20: Error writing to floppy! The floppy is defective. This volume will be rewritten on a new floppy. Remove floppy before attempting to continue.

The most likely problem is a damaged disk or the wrong disk type for the drive, although this could also be caused by the wrong DMA speed setting, an incorrect drive definition or a hardware fault. Try changing the disk and then continuing the operation. If the disk is at fault, the operation will proceed from the beginning of the defective volume.

### 21: Error reading from floppy! The floppy is defective.

Any lost data will not be recovered, but you can press SPACE BAR to continue the restore and FASTBACK PLUS will restore the damaged file as best it can and then continue with the rest of the files on this disk.

### 22: Fatal error during hardware test! Unable to complete test.

If the floppy disk you are using for the test is not damaged, improperly inserted, or the wrong type for the drive, you can try restarting the test at a slower DMA speed.

### 23: Unable to locate [FILENAME]! Unable to complete test.

Probably a mistyped file or path name.

### 24: File length incorrect for [FILENAME]! Unable to complete test.

The file you're working with may not be the named file.

### 25: Floppy drive hardware not defined!  Unable to complete test.

You have incorrectly defined the floppy drive.

### 26: Floppy drive conflicts with startup drive!  Backup history will not be created.

You may not have properly installed FASTBACK PLUS, or you may be logged in to the wrong drive.

### 27: Unrecoverable error reading from floppy! This floppy is defective. Ready to attempt continuation.

Try another diskette.

### 28: Waiting for confirmation of disk switch! Continue after switching floppy disks.

FASTBACK PLUS is waiting for you to switch disks.

### 29: This disk already contains data. Please confirm overwrite or retry with a new disk.

Either switch to an unused disk or confirm that FASTBACK PLUS may overwrite the data on the current disk.

### 40: Unable to open backup destination!

The backup disk may be write-protected or may be improperly inserted.

### 41: Unable to open history file!

Your hard disk may be full. Try removing some files.

### 42: Unable to change to path [PATHNAME]!

If you are on a network computer, this path may only be accessible from a higher security level than you have. If not, your hard disk may be damaged. FASTBACK PLUS continues, after a brief pause, with the next pathname.

### 43: Unable to open file [FILENAME] for backup! Continuing with next file.

If you are on a network computer, this file may only be accessible from a higher security level than you have. If not, your hard disk may be damaged. FASTBACK PLUS continues, after a brief pause, with the next filename.

### 44: Error while reading file [FILENAME]! Continuing with next file.

FASTBACK PLUS aborts operations on this file and continues with the next file.

### 45: Failure while writing to destination file [FILENAME]!

The destination disk may be damaged; try replacing it.

### 46: Unable to copy history file to backup set!

The disk may be full or damaged.

### 47: Maximum subdirectory depth exceeded. Files below this level will not be processed.

The maximum subdirectory depth is 16, including the root directory.

### 48: WARNING! Writing to 40 track disks in an 80 track drive. Do not use disks previously written or formatted by a 40 track drive. Start with new or magnetically bulk erased disks.

FASTBACK PLUS is just reminding you that you must use new diskettes when writing a 40 track format on 80 track diskettes.

### 49: Failure compressing file data! Attempting to continue.

A rare message—it means that FASTBACK PLUS's data compression routines are failing somehow. You should contact Technical Support at Fifth Generation Systems. Meanwhile, you can change the Compression of Data setting on the Advanced Options menu to Off and restart the backup.

### 50: Failure updating the volume number continuity file! the backup data remains unaffected by this error, and is still good.

FASTBACK PLUS was unable to record this volume number in the backup history file. Make a note of it.

### 51: Failure appending history file to the history file from the full backup! The backup data remains unaffected by this error, and is still good.

FASTBACK PLUS was unable to append the incremental history file to the last full history file. Make a note of it.

**52: Failure deleting old history files for this drive! The data on the backup set is not affected by this error. You may wish to delete old history files using the DOS ERASE command.**

You can always delete old history files with the DOS ERASE command.

**60: Failure while reading from [FILENAME]!**

The DOS restore source file FASTBACK PLUS is trying to read may be damaged; note the filename.

**61: Unknown record type encountered! Attempting to continue.**

The disk may be damaged. Note the filename.

**62: Invalid record length encountered! Attempting to continue.**

The disk may be damaged. Note the filename.

**63: Unable to restore file [FILENAME]! Continuing with the next file.**

Probably a system file. FASTBACK PLUS will not restore system files.

**64: Failure while writing file contents! Attempting to continue with next file.**

Your hard disk may be full or damaged. Try removing some files.

**65: Failure expanding compressed file data! Attempting to continue.**

The backup disk may be damaged. Note the filename.

**66: Failure expanding compressed file data! Length mismatch. Attempting to continue.**

The backup disk may be damaged. Note the filename.

**67: Failure reading compressed file data! Packet number mismatch! Attempting to continue.**

Either the disk is damaged, or you have inserted disks out of volume-sequence. Note the filename.

**68: Failure preparing volume prompting list! Continuing without smart volume prompting. Insert the backup volumes in numerical order.**

FASTBACK PLUS is unable to conduct a smart restore based on history file information. It will prompt for sequential disk switching instead.

**69: This volume is not the next one in sequence! Retry with the correct volume, or confirm turning off the smart volume prompting.**

You inserted the wrong disk during a smart restore. If you proceed with this disk, FASTBACK PLUS will revert to sequential prompting for disks for the remainder of the restore.

**70: The free space on the hard disk is too small to accommodate the restore files!**

Either make more room on your hard disk, or edit your include files list to reduce the number of files to restore.

**71: Failure attempting to change to, and then to create, path [PATHNAME]! Will attempt to continue, but some files may not be restored to their original subdirectories.**

FASTBACK PLUS was unable to restore some files to their original sub-directory. Note that there may be inconsistencies in the directory structure of your restored files.

**72: The file [FILENAME] already exists on the hard disk, and is marked as a System file! It will not be overwritten, in order to avoid potential DOS boot problems. Continuing with the next file.**

FASTBACK PLUS will not restore system files.

**73: The file [FILENAME] already exists on the hard disk, and is marked as a Hidden or Read Only file! Please confirm overwrite, or continue with the next file.**

To overwrite Hidden or Read Only files, FASTBACK PLUS requires your confirmation.

### 80: Insufficient memory for directory display! Directory not available.

Not enough memory is available to construct the requested directory tree. Try removing some of your memory resident programs.

### 81: Directory display file limit exceeded. Some files will not be displayed.

FASTBACK PLUS can only display a maximum of 4,096 files in a directory listing. Files exceeding that limit will be backed up and restored, but not displayed in the directory.

### 82: Too many directories! Some directories will not be displayed.

FASTBACK PLUS can only display up to 200 directories and subdirectories.

### 83: Insufficient memory or COMMAND.COM not found! Cannot shell to MS-DOS.

Not enough memory is available to run MS-DOS commands from FASTBACK PLUS. Try removing some memory resident programs. (This error may also indicate that FASTBACK PLUS could not locate COMMAND.COM and therefore could not run the command.

### 84: Unable to locate history files in [SUPPORT DIRECTORY]! Restore directory not available.

The history files are not where FASTBACK PLUS expects them to be. Try using **Get History** from the Restore Progress menu to locate the file.

### 90: Invalid data entry! Please answer 'Y' for yes or 'N' for no.

You were prompted to enter Y or N, but you entered something else.

### 91: Invalid directory name! Must begin with \.

You forgot to precede a directory name with the required \ character.

**92: Invalid filespec! Must not contain \.**

A filename cannot contain the \ character.

**93: File specification list is full! Insert operation aborted.**

The Include or Exclude Files list can only contain up to 20 pathnames. Try doing your backup or restore procedure in smaller chunks.

**94: Batch operation suspended!**

The batch file may contain incorrectly specified commands, or the commands may be given in an unacceptable order.

**95: You have commanded a backup identical to one just completed! Please confirm you wish to perform the backup again.**

You may have pressed ENTER at Start Backup, thinking you were at Quit.

**96: You have commanded a restore identical to the one just completed! Please confirm you wish to perform the restore again.**

You may have pressed ENTER at Start Restore, thinking you were at Quit.

# *Glossary*

**Backup**  A copy of a file, directory or disk that you make as a safeguard against loss or damage to your data.

**Back up**  The process of making a backup.

**Buffer**  A segment of memory that a program sets aside to use as a temporary storage area during a procedure.

**Default**  A setting or action that a program tells the computer to use unless or until it receives other instructions from the user.

**Default Directory**  The directory indicated by the current DOS prompt. To change the default directory, use the DOS CD command.

**Differential Backup**  A backup of all files that have changed since the last full backup of these files, regardless of whether they have been backed up in an interim differential backup.

**Disk Drive**  The device that reads information from and writes information to either a hard disk (built-in) or a floppy disk.

**Disk**   A magnetically coated storage device for computer data. Can be either a hard disk, which is built in to your computer, or a floppy disk, which you insert and remove.

**Diskette**   A floppy disk.

**DOS**   Stands for Disk Operating System. If you use an IBM or compatible personal computer, your operating system is MS-DOS.

**DOS Pathname**   DOS divides a hard disk up into *directories*, which may contain one or more *subdirectories*, each containing one or more *files*. A DOS *pathname* is simply the way that DOS spells out where it is storing a certain portion of your data: in a file, which resides in a directory, which may or may not be a subdirectory of a higher-level directory, which resides on a particular disk or drive. A DOS pathname always names the drive first, then the directory and any subdirectories, all divided by \ characters, and finally the filename. For example, the pathname C:\BUSINESS\SPREADSHEETS\MONTHLY\MARCH.FIN specifies a file named MARCH.FIN, which resides in a directory named \MONTHLY, which is a subdirectory of \SPREADSHEETS, which, in turn, is a subdirectory of \BUSINESS, which resides in the root directory on the C drive.

**Floppy**   A floppy, or removable, disk used in the A or B drive of your computer.

**Hard Disk**   The built-in large capacity disk (usually 10mb or larger) used as a permanent storage device for your computer programs and data.

**Incremental Backup**   A partial backup that backs up all files that have changed since the last incremental backup.

**Logical Device**   Part of a computer that works as an equivalent to another part, specifically refers to storage devices, or drives.

**Memory Resident Program**   A utility program—such as a "desktop" calendar, notepad or calculator program, or a "screen dump" program—which is typically installed when you start your computer up, and remains in memory (taking up space!) even when you are actively using another program.

**Menu**   A graphically displayed listing of commands or settings for a computer program. FASTBACK PLUS relies heavily on menus.

**Pathname**   See DOS Pathname.

**Root Directory**   The top-most directory on your hard disk, created by DOS and designated simply by a \. All named directories are subdirectories of the root directory.

**Support Directory**   The directory that you have installed all the FAST-BACK PLUS program files into. When you install FASTBACK PLUS, \FASTBACK is the default name suggested for this support directory.

**Volume**   The name that FASTBACK PLUS uses to refer to a single floppy disk out of a whole backup set: Volume 1, Volume 2, etc.

**Wildcard Designation (or String)**   A character sequence (*.*) that DOS allows you to use when you want to specify "any file (or directory) with this name or file extension". Can be used whole to specify all files in the named directory (*.*), or in part to specify "all files with this name" (NAME.*) or "all files with this file extension" (*.EXT).

# *Tips for Users of FASTBACK and FASTBACK II*

## Using FASTBACK PLUS from DOS

Although FASTBACK PLUS offers many new features and an easy user interface, users of the original FASTBACK may prefer to continue using the old interaction style.

After installing FASTBACK PLUS using the instructions in Appendix A, you can activate and use FASTBACK PLUS from the DOS command line by executing FASTBACK.EXE.

First, change your default directory to the directory where you installed FASTBACK PLUS (CD\[directory name]).

Then type FASTBACK and press ENTER.

FASTBACK.EXE offers an old-style prompting interface to guide you through making backups without using the FASTBACK PLUS menu system. This interface has some significant additions to the old FASTBACK. You can now choose to:

- Estimate the time and disks required for a backup before executing it.
- Specify exiting to DOS when your backup is completed.
- ESC back through prompts to edit your responses before proceeding.

Pressing ENTER at the last prompt will begin the backup procedure you have specified with your responses.

## Using Old Batch Files with FASTBACK PLUS

You can still use your old FASTBACK batch files with FASTBACK PLUS. They will execute the specified procedures without modification, using FASTBACK PLUS settings.

You can also enter FASTBACK PLUS commands directly from the DOS command line. See Chapter 12 for information about the automation possibilities in FASTBACK PLUS.

## Restoring Macintosh Backups Made with FASTBACK II

FASTBACK PLUS can restore backups made on a Macintosh computer with FASTBACK II—but you must first convert the files to a format acceptable to MS-DOS.

To convert your Macintosh backup stream to a DOS file, you can use one of the following conversion programs:

- Apple File Exchange, v. 1.1.1 or later, from the Macintosh Utilities Disk 2 (System version 6.0.3 or later)
- TOPS
- Rapport
- DOSMounter

Once your Macintosh backup is converted to a DOS file, you must use the DOS REN command to rename each backup stream file to a DOS filename. Use the following naming convention:

```
[FILENAME].001
[FILENAME].002
[FILENAME].003
```

and so on. [FILENAME] should be different for each backup set and must be exactly eight characters long. The file extensions must enumerate the backup sets, beginning with .001, as in the examples above.

You may find it convenient to use the same naming convention that FASTBACK PLUS uses, for example:

```
C900514A.001
```

where C represents the hard disk backed up, 900514 represents the date of the backup (May 14th, 1990 in this case), and A indicates that this was the first backup of that drive made on this date.

### Restoring the Converted Files

To restore converted Macintosh backups, follow the procedure outlined in Chapter 8, except that you must select **Regular DOS Drive and Path** as the **Restore Source**. When you do so, a window appears at the bottom of the screen for you to enter the correct pathname as follows:

1. Type in the correct drive and directory to restore the converted file from (for example, A:\)
2. Press TAB to move over to the **Backup Set Name:** field.
3. Enter the filename that you gave the file when you converted it. (If you can't remember the filename, press F3 to get a directory listing, press TAB to go to the accompanying files window, highlight the correct filename, and press INS.)
4. Press ESC to return to the Main FASTBACK PLUS Restore menu, and then proceed with the restore.

### Filename Reconciliation

FASTBACK PLUS automatically reconciles the inherent differences between Macintosh filenames and DOS filenames as follows:

1. FASTBACK PLUS strips out any of the special characters allowed
   in Macintosh names that are not allowed in DOS names: ? , * / [ ]
   \ ; " =

2. FASTBACK PLUS makes the necessary adjustments to shorten
   Macintosh filenames to an acceptable DOS length and use DOS
   pathname syntax. DOS pathnames may *total* up to 66 characters,
   but file and directory names may not exceed eight characters, plus
   a 3-character extension. And DOS uses the backslash (\) character
   as a directory name delimiter. So, for example, the Macintosh
   filename

   ```
   DIREC1;DIREC1_SUBDIR2;DIREC3;letter to Mary
   ```

   becomes the DOS filename

   ```
   \DIREC1\DIREC1_S\DIREC3\LETTERTO.MAR.
   ```

3. FASTBACK PLUS ignores the Macintosh "resource fork" of the
   filename, and uses only the "data fork". The data fork contains the
   text information, which is what FASTBACK PLUS restores.

# *Index*

## A

Archive Flag 12, 17, 19, 53, 65, 92
    and incremental/differential backups 13-16
    and its menu 75-76
Archiving 7
Audible Prompts 18, 82, 101-102, 153
AUTOEXEC.BAT file 193, 203

## B

Backups
    Backup menu 9, 53, 55-56, 127, 136
    differential 34, 56
    and Exclude Files, 53, 59, 136

    full 11, 105, 113
    incremental 34, 56
    and the Macintosh 220
    partial 11, 13, 121-122
    Start Backup 53, 62
    strategy 33
    types 11-12, 15-16, 19, 34, 55-58, 67, 76, 122
    and user levels 18-19
Batch files 164, 170
    defined 159-160
    executing from DOS command line 167
    and old files, 220

## C

Characters
    asterisk 27
    wildcard 27